I0438670

Avoiding the Hatchet Man
PRACTICAL ADVICE FOR THE EMPLOYED AND UNEMPLOYED

By

Patrick Connor

Eloquent Books

Copyright 2009

All rights reserved – Patrick Connor

No part of this book may be reproduced or transmitted in any form or by any means, graphic, electronic, or mechanical, including photocopying, recording, taping, or by any information storage retrieval system, without the permission, in writing, from the publisher.

Eloquent Books
An imprint of Strategic Book Group
P.O. Box 333
Durham CT 06422
www.StrategicBookGroup.com

ISBN: 978-1-60911-044-4

Printed in the United States of America

Book Design: SP

This book is designed to provide accurate and authoritative information in regard to the subject matter covered. It is sold with the understanding that the publisher is not engaged in rendering legal, accounting, or other professional services. If legal advice or other expert assistance is required, the service of a competent professional person should be sought.

From a Declaration of Principles Jointly Adopted by a Committee of the American Bar Association and a Committee of Publishers and Associations

Disclaimer required by Texas statutes:

This product is not a substitute for legal advice.

DEDICATION

I dedicate this undertaking to my family who has provided me with endless support and encouragement. Specifically, my wife (Tina) and our four boys (Mitch, Grant, Reed, and Kent) have been inspirational to me during difficult times and significant travels. They have made my life rewarding in every respect. When they reflect back on their lives, I can only hope that I played a role in helping them to have a rewarding life as well.

I additionally dedicate this book to my extended family. Each has shown me in everyday life the meaning of words that otherwise would have only been terms in the dictionary. Madlyn, my mom, exemplifies compassion. Bill, my father, stands for integrity. My brother, Bill, personifies zeal. Marge, my mother-in-law, models composure. Last but not least, my father-in-law, Charlie, demonstrates perspective. Thanks to each of them for being who they are.

ACKNOWLEDGEMENTS

Admittedly, my line of work can leave a bad taste in the mouths of some or evoke scorn and contempt from others. However, I believe my professional approach, coupled with an empathetic attitude, allows those involved to retain their integrity, self-worth, and confidence. They can walk with their heads held high and can continue to consider themselves as valuable to the job market. This is comforting to me because bad things often happen to good people through no fault of their own.

I have always lived by the credo that if you don't continue to develop your skills, you will vanish into extinction like the dinosaurs. Therefore, in my professional career, I sought out individuals I knew I could learn from. The fact that they were mentoring me was sometimes clear; at other times, it may not have been as apparent. Each was responsible in his or her own way for advancing my knowledge, skills, and abilities to the next level. More importantly, each shaped my softer skills, including my attitude, work ethic, communication skills, and overall professionalism.

I have worn many hats in my career as I meandered in and out of virtually every sector of business. In each sector, I was fortunate to work with several individuals who shined through as the best of the best. I would be remiss if I didn't acknowledge them here, as they have helped me become who I am today.

In the nonprofit field, I would like to thank Joe Burke, George Hansen, Rich Jackson, Claudia Kurianowicz, and Al Madden. They showed me how integrity and compassion play a significant role in dealing with others in the workplace, particularly when making decisions involving individuals or businesses that are already experiencing difficulties.

In the governmental sector, I need to thank Dan Fewkes and Ken Zuhlke. They demonstrated what it truly means to be a public servant. Despite enormous workplace pressures that resulted when the State of Illinois failed to approve a budget because of feuding legislators,

Dan and Ken were rock solid in their attitude and performance. The government would be wise to appropriate funds to clone these two gentlemen.

As for the public sector, Warren Grayson, Mia Igyarto, and Patty Sellergren taught me how the fields of employment law and human resources can be combined to create a tapestry of art. They helped me understand how this combined art could then be used to promote fairness for the workforce and profits for the shareholders.

For the private sector, William Cavanagh, Amy Doan, and Mike O'Leary are business owners who keep me energized and optimistic. They have each marked a place in their communities and beyond through smarts, hard work, guts, and true grit. For me, these individuals are figuratively the face of the American spirit. Like other business owners across the country, they are passionate about their companies. They awake each day ready to tackle the challenges of running a business 24/7/365. A new word should be coined to describe business owners; the innocent and whimsical word *entrepreneur* seems almost insulting.

Last but not least, I thank Ed Matushek for being my first mentor in my professional career. Without his abundance of confidence in me so early in my career, I am certain that I would not have been such a risk taker throughout my entire life. He shaped my career more than he will ever know. In fact, I probably owe to him that I even wrote this book.

All the individuals named above earned and deserve my respect. However, because they were not involved in the writing of this book and will read it for the first time simultaneously with the general public, I take full responsibility for any ideas you might disagree with.

Finally, I would like to thank several public libraries for offering me a quiet haven to work on this book. Each of them is staffed with extremely knowledgeable and friendly librarians (with a special shout out to Bill Black and his keen sense of humor):

Vernon Area Public Library
300 Olde Half Day Road
Lincolnshire, IL 60069
www.vapld.info

McHenry Public Library
809 N. Front St. (Route 31)
McHenry, IL 60050
www.mchenrylibrary.org

Arlington Heights Memorial
Library
500 N. Dunton Avenue
Arlington Heights, IL 60004
www.ahml.info

Mount Prospect Public
Library
10 South Emerson Street
Mount Prospect, IL 60056
www.mppl.org

CONTENTS

THE HATCHET MAN COMETH

CHAPTER 1

LAYOFF HAPPENS

The global economy is in trouble. The United States economy is suffering. According to the television news anchors, radio talk show hosts, and newspaper headlines, the economic downturn remains stubborn, and unemployment will continue to climb for at least the foreseeable future.

Hitting closer to home, the company you work for is in turmoil as well. You and your peers have been required to take unpaid furlough days. The words "bonus" and "raise" are no longer part of the company vocabulary. The last time a peer mentioned these taboo words at a meeting they were met with a quick and decisive response from management. The response was "you're lucky you have a job." Since that day, no one at your company has dared to mutter those words again. Now there is a disturbing rumor circulating that there will be layoffs on Friday. You hope it is just a rumor. Your manager will neither confirm nor deny the veracity of the rumor.

On Thursday morning, your manager calls everyone in your department into the training room for an impromptu meeting. This development results in you immediately experiencing adverse physical reactions. Your stomach starts to gurgle, your neck stiffens, and your chest twinges with tightness. You leave the crowd walking down the hall and turn into the bathroom momentarily where you experience the dry heaves. As you try to regain your composure, tears well up in your eyes, and you begin to shake with nervousness. Thoughts of panic flash through your mind, including how to tell your spouse that you were laid off and how you won't be able to pay your rent or mortgage. If only you had a rainy day fund to fall back on. As you hurry down the hall to catch up with your peers who are turning into the training room, you begin to grow angry. It just isn't fair for the company to let you go. You recall things that you have done in the past that showed your loyalty. Just last year, you rescheduled a planned vacation when the company landed an unexpected, large customer order. Additionally, you always finish your projects on time—well, almost every time. You never took so much as a company pen home without permission. You've done nothing to warrant this treatment.

You enter the training room, and the air is thick with stress and nervous perspiration. Your manager is standing in the front of the room next to the company's human resources director, who is sitting. The meeting begins with your manager saying in a shaky voice, "All right, everyone, sit down and let's get this over." Your stomach flips again. The employee next to you groans, and your work partner of five years, who is sitting behind you, says in a low but clear voice, "Oh, shit!" The human resources director stands slowly and speaks in a firm voice. She states, "It has come to management's attention that a rumor is circulating about layoffs." The room gets deftly quiet. She continues on to note that the rumor is beginning to hurt productivity and that it must stop. After everyone realizes that the meeting is not a layoff announcement, the tension in the room starts to subside. You and your coworkers sigh in relief and basically tune out the remainder of the human resources director's comments.

The human resources director stops speaking and asks if there are any questions. The youngest employee in your department is bold and speaks up. He challenges the human resources director for more information and asks point-blank if there is any truth to the layoff rumor. Your manager steps in and says, "Even if it is true, do you really think the company will tell you before it is ready?" While you and your peers are not content with that answer, you all know that what the manager said is true, and no one pushes further for an answer. The meeting ends, and everyone is told to return to work. The hallway talk on return is somewhat upbeat. After all, if layoffs were imminent, the meeting certainly would not have been held. You go home that night and tell your spouse and friends about what occurred that day, and you share your cautious optimism about having job security.

The next day goes just like every Friday since you started working there. That is, until your work partner stops by a half hour before quitting time and says, "Let's go. We'll be late." "Late for what?" you respond. "The meeting in the training room," he replies. You stare at him with a clueless face. With a look of terror, he responds, "Weren't you told to attend this meeting?" As you shake your head to indicate no, you see half of your department coworkers heading down the hall toward the training room. You swallow to moisten your parched mouth. In the most upbeat tone that you can mustard under the situation, you tell your partner, "I am sure you will be fine. Call me tonight when you get home."

No call comes that night. You call him Saturday morning, and your beliefs are confirmed. Half of the department, including your work partner, was let go. They were required to clean out their personal belongings last night. You try to comfort your friend. With feigned sincerity, you note that he is probably better off without the company because the job wasn't that good in the first place. You state that the layoff is probably a blessing in disguise, and you're confident that he will find a position with a better company. Several minutes later, you hang up the telephone. Your mind goes into overdrive. Your coworker was as good a worker as you, perhaps even better. Why is he gone, and you're not? Will you be so fortunate as to survive the next round of layoffs? Is there anything you could do to better position yourself to survive another wave of layoffs? What should you be doing just in case you are called into the training room next time? What would you do if you were laid off? What would happen to you and your family's health insurance benefits? You are riddled with questions but have no answers.

After the shock wears off, you start to reflect on whether there was something you did differently than your peers. Your work productivity, ethics, and loyalty to the company don't seem to set you apart. Nonetheless, there has to be something that allowed you to be spared from the wrath of the hatchet man. If you could pinpoint what it is, then you could duplicate it and perhaps increase your chances of avoiding the hatchet man when the next round of layoffs come.

Your thought process is correct. You did do something to save your job. However, unless you are an expert with layoffs, people management, human nature and employment laws, it is highly improbable that you will analyze the situation correctly so that you can repeat your efforts. This is where I come in. I am a professional hatchet man and have been for more than twenty years. My role is to oversee the integrity and legal compliance of company layoffs. In other words, I need to ensure that the individuals identified for a layoff are selected fairly and according to objective criteria so that the company's action is legally defendable. Over the years, I have seen an infinite number of ways that business leaders and managers attempt to get around the objective criteria and hand pick which employees keep their jobs. Nonetheless, I have found that there is a predictable method to their madness. I explain their madness and offer suggestions on how to use it against them and heighten your chances of keeping your job. This book will serve as a road map for individuals like you and your laid-off work partner to follow during the nerve-racking journey. This book begins with tips for avoiding the hatchet man and ends with advice about fighting your company for what is rightfully yours if the hatchet man should catch you.

In the next chapter, I explain how the discussions that are presently occurring in your company's boardroom concerning job eliminations are virtually identical to those that I have been involved with in companies scattered throughout the United States over the past two decades. It is irrelevant whether the job eliminations topic is driven by poor economic times or by a financially struggling company in prosperous times. While companies consult with professionals proactively to ensure the integrity of the job elimination process, the process is never truly bulletproof because there are people involved. Where there are people, there are human emotions and fears and, thus, a weak link. In disclosing closely held secrets, I discuss how you can exploit the human emotions and fears of your manager to influence the job elimination process and potentially save your job.

Rule of Thumb
You don't survive a round of job eliminations based on luck. While layoffs happen every day, you need not be a sitting duck and wait for your turn. You need to develop and implement a plan of action to influence your destiny and increase your chances of staying employed.

CHAPTER 2

CLOSELY HELD SECRETS REVEALED

I have seen countless people lose their jobs when profits start to shrink and sales decline. Sometimes it is the result of an economic downturn, increased competition in the marketplace, or the result of an inept CEO who had no vision for the company's future. Of course, there were more than a few times when it was simply a way for a high-ranking member of management to make room for a relative, a friend, or the like. When job eliminations are required, companies turn to me for guidance.

My experience deems me a war veteran in counseling anxiety-stricken corporate leaders and managers in difficult economic times. Over the years, I have seen many well-tempered business leaders lose control of their emotions and require restraining in the corporate boardroom. More than one senior manager has broken down in tears in front of me. One executive even asked me for forgiveness for the actions that needed to be taken. My experiences stop just short of coaxing a CEO to come in off an office window ledge.

I am not a trained psychologist; I am a corporate attorney with specialized training in human resources management. To the businesses that utilize my services, I am known as the hatchet man. I am good at what I do. I make a comfortable living and make no apologies for performing the services requested. My role is to help strong companies become stronger, struggling companies survive, and failing companies remain viable while seeking financing or a new owner. In my view, I help breathe life into companies. Workforces view me differently.

Regardless of the reason I am brought on board, the end result is the same: a person, department, or company site will suffer job elimination. To employees losing their jobs, the reason for the company's action is immaterial. A valid business justification for the job eliminations does not help the impacted individuals put food on the table or pay their mortgages. And, by the way, do not be fooled by the media; the small amount that individuals get from their state unemployment office is not enough to keep their lives from unraveling.

Practical Advice Only

Like a magician who reveals his secrets, I provide information that companies do not want you to know and that my peers refuse to share without charging exorbitant consulting fees. Some information may seem commonsensical. If so, I accomplished my goal of avoiding unnecessary and boring discussions concerning the legal underpinnings of my thoughts. My advice is also intended to be practical and void of any academic theories espoused by college professors, recruiters, headhunters, and outplacement representatives. I strive to give you only what you want and need to immediately become proactive at work, take control of your destiny, and foil the hatchet man's efforts at eliminating your job.

You are confronted with choices every day that you show up to work. How you respond to these choices shapes your career path. In difficult economic times, your responses often determine if you stay employed or join the masses entering the surreal world of unemployment. Throughout this book, I recount numerous real-life stories that highlight choices that were handled properly and saved an individual's job. I also discuss how some individuals failed to identify these choices as potential stumbling blocks and responded poorly, sabotaging their careers and losing their jobs.

This book shares my experiences and insights acquired through conversations with and observations of business leaders, company managers, and employees who have gone through the job elimination process. It provides suggestions and guidelines on three main topics:

- How to improve your chances of avoiding the hatchet man and remaining employed through proven strategies and techniques;
- How to implement a proactive plan while you are still employed to increase your chances of finding alternative employment should your job be eliminated; and
- A simple process to help you make informed and timely decisions about COBRA, alternative health insurance, your legal rights against the company, and whether you should sign a severance document in the event your job is eliminated.

18

While no book can explain every employment relationship, my personal experiences are broad and stem from private, public, governmental, and nonprofit organizations in the professional, service, manufacturing, and retail industries. I have learned that managers are individuals who react in a predictable manner during difficult times regardless of the company's sector or industry. Therefore, my suggestions are equally applicable to the chemical worker in San Jose, the governmental accountant in Cleveland, the clothes sales associate in Nashville, or the site manager of a gasket factory in Philadelphia. On the other hand, this book is equally beneficial to business leaders of organizations ranging in size from family owned businesses to multinational corporations. Business leaders need to understand how the thought process of their managers changes during troubled times. Without a firm grasp of the predictable behaviors and changing attitudes of company managers during periods of unrest, successful change implementation, such as a reduction in workforce, is unlikely.

Because the pivotal person to any layoff plan and to your job security is your company manager, you need to first determine what motivates him or her and what drives his or her decisions. Only then can a plan of action be developed to demonstrate that you are a go-to employee who should be retained. In the next chapter, I discuss what universally drives a company manager and how to prey on this fear for your own benefit.

Rule of Thumb
No matter how diligent a company is about ensuring the integrity and fairness of the job elimination process, it is still a manual process involving humans who are driven by emotion and fear. By exploiting this understanding, you can behave in an orchestrated manner that could positively influence any company decision regarding your job security.

KEEPING YOUR JOB

CHAPTER 3

PREY ON YOUR MANAGER'S FEARS

Companies stopped looking out for the good of their employees decades ago. Because of this, employees change jobs in their careers more than ever before in an effort to take care of themselves. This is not a breakthrough revelation but a fact of life.

What should you do when the economy in general deteriorates and jobs are scarce? In this situation, you need to figure out how to control your present work environment and strengthen your job security. Based on my experiences, I contend that you can in fact protect your job after you understand the fears of your manager. Fortunately, managers become predictable when job eliminations start to be implemented.

Loyalty to Whom?

Every time I plan a reduction in workforce, I am reminded that there are no loyal company managers still in existence. Individuals fitting the old stereotype of the loyal company manager are now extinct. They have been replaced by a new generation of managers who are consumed with their own best interests. Armed with this knowledge, you can make strategic decisions that will separate you from your peers and improve your chances of remaining employed.

Most managers work their way up the corporate ladder by playing within the company's rules. They may play some corporate politics to help with a promotion, but they generally play within the rules established by the company, strive to reach the company's goals, and comply with the laws that govern the employment relationship. It is easy to be the perfect company manager when economic times are good.

When the economy gets tough and job eliminations commence, the priorities and goals of company managers change and not for the better. Unlike previous generations, managers today shed their loyalties to the company and focus on their own job security. This is only natural when you take into account that managers today

23

lose their jobs every bit as fast as—if not faster—than their direct reports. Managers have mortgages, bills, and families just like everyone else. The shift of the managers' priorities plays a significant role in clouding the managers' thinking in the best interest of the company.

Risky Maneuvers

While working with managers on the details of job eliminations, I explain that there are certain guidelines that need to be adhered to in the decision-making process. For instance, I oversee the development of elaborate job evaluation matrices that in theory remove all subjectivity from the decision making. By eliminating subjectivity, a bulletproof process is created for identifying the individuals who will be eliminated. This is important if a terminated employee seeks to challenge the decision in court.

Regardless of the fairness of the process developed, managers blatantly try to get around the system. They do everything they can to bypass the objectivity safeguards and control the outcome based on nothing more than subjectivity. The creative methods in which managers try to accomplish their goals know no bounds. For our purposes, their methods are irrelevant, but the reason they take such risk is of the utmost importance.

Early in my career, I thought managers were trying to protect the jobs of their friends. If not, I assumed that they were trying to take care of employees who were hard workers or perhaps yes-employees who brought the manager lunch twice a week. While this may be true when the economy is strong and promotions are being considered, I learned that nothing could be further from the truth in difficult times.

The pattern eventually became crystal clear to me regarding who managers thought were worthy of such a risk. It was not their friends or the yes-employees but rather employees who were viewed by the managers as being loyal to them personally. These employees were viewed by the managers as willing to do what was necessary to help the managers achieve their own personal goal of remaining employed. Managers are willing to risk everything to save employees who are loyal to them. This is because managers believe they will lose their jobs subsequently anyway without these employees.

Unlike past generations, managers today are generally responsible for picking up the additional work after the job eliminations. Based on these increased work responsibilities and the knowledge that managers tend to be laid off in a subsequent wave of job eliminations, managers shed their loyalties to the company. Their natural instinct of survival kicks in, and they focus on only one self-serving goal: self-preservation.

Managers view their company goals as too abstract and too far off to save their jobs. They feel a sense of urgency in turning their priorities to goals that can be achieved quickly before the next wave of job eliminations are announced. Throughout this book, I explain how to increase your chances of staying employed by seeking out opportunities to demonstrate yourself as an employee loyal to your manager.

Work Smarter or Harder?

During the two decades in which I was the mastermind and bearer of bad news involving job eliminations, I gained insight into how things could have worked out differently for the employees selected for job termination through observation and discussions with managers and displaced employees. I developed an understanding of how an employee who received good performance reviews, including in some instances one not more than a few weeks beforehand, could be identified as an employee who is deadweight and needs to be eliminated. What could the employee have done differently? Why was this employee selected for elimination out a group of peers?

Many of us heard the time-tested adage "work smarter not harder." How does that reconcile with the other adage: "keep your nose to the grindstone"? I contend that the two adages are not inconsistent and can be reconciled. There is a subtle but monumental underpinning in common between the two. According to either adage, you need to work hard to accomplish your goal: in this case, to remain employed. The only difference is that an assumption is commonly read into the latter adage that requires you to work hard for the company. However, the second adage does not actually state on whose behalf you should be working. Collectively, the adages imply that if you want to accomplish your goals, you need to work hard and be smart about where you focus your efforts. For our purposes here, you should work hard at figuring out the best way to accomplish your goal of remaining employed.

In the following chapters, I discuss techniques to assist you in becoming smarter in the workplace and thereby improve your chances of remaining employed. These techniques stress the importance of devoting your attention and time to shaping your manager's perception of you with the objective of being perceived as an asset to your manager rather than to the company.

Conscientious work accompanied with a solid work ethic will typically keep you employed in a good economy. The same is not true in poor economic times when job eliminations are aplenty. If you don't believe me, spend an afternoon at your local unemployment office and listen to the repetitive complaints from displaced workers about how they gave their souls to the company. Hard work that is misplaced begets no reward. This book attempts to open your eyes and provide you with common sense ideas about how to control your destiny in the workplace. Otherwise, you may suffer a fate of unemployment at the hands of the hatchet man.

Rule of Thumb
If you want to save your job, you need to view the world from the perspective of your manager. You must vigilantly look for and exploit opportunities to demonstrate that you are primarily a valuable asset to your manager and secondarily to the company.

CHAPTER 4

STRESS-INDUCED MONSTERS

A true but adapted story:

After undergoing several waves of layoffs over a two-year period, the company I was working with was experiencing poor morale. There was no disputing that the anxiety level was high in the workforce. Management firmly believed that their remaining employees were looking for new jobs. Employees held their breath at every staff meeting for fear that the next layoff would be announced. It was at this troubled company that I learned of a bizarre personality shift that occurred with one of its employees.

Apparently, a ten-year employee in the procurement department struggled to contain her normal professional demeanor in the midst of the uncertainty. She was described as a friendly woman who was devoted to her family and her five young children. With each passing month, this individual's frustration grew, and her personality began to change for the worse. Although she was always a quiet individual, she became almost reclusive at work. According to her peers and manager, they knew that her personality transformation climaxed when she vividly described a dream she had with her peers. The anxiety-stricken employee explained that she had dreamt that she walked into her manager's office and turned in her resignation. She continued on to say that while she was walking to her car in the dream, she threw a hazard flare through the manager's car window and watched the car burn while she stood there and laughed. I was told that at first there was an uncomfortable laugh by some of her peers, and then an eerie silence took over.

Fortunately for this individual, the next round of job eliminations occurred almost a year after she shared her dream. She was let go at that time. Prior to the stress-induced personality transformation, there was no reason for this employee to be terminated. In fact, based on her likeability over the previous ten years, no one in the company even thought to suspend her, pending a fitness-for-duty exam. Whether right or wrong, management interpreted the dream as only an indication that she was disenchanted with the company and not as a premonition of workplace violence. In fact, her productivity never suffered, and she was viewed as one of the best employees in that department right up to the day she was laid off.

***

Don't Be Perceived as a Yes-Man

First, a word of caution about trying to save your job by applying the techniques explained in this book or any other techniques you develop on your own. You must be cognizant of how you are perceived by your manager while implementing the techniques. Even if the techniques take you out of your comfort zone, your approach and attitude has to be real and believable for it to be successful. Lucky for you, the personalities of everyone in the workplace undergo stress-induced changes during difficult times. The personality changes of your peers will mask your changed behavior while implementing calculated efforts to improve your job security. The most important thing about applying the techniques in this book is that your actions and words be perceived as genuine. This should not be hard to accomplish because your goal truthfully is to save your job.

Stress causes an individual's personality and demeanor to become exaggerated. Exaggeration of any personality type, especially when left unchecked, can lead to undesirable consequences. From my experience, the demeanors of employees with specific personality types change in somewhat predictable but problematic ways after prolonged stress.

Type A Personality Individuals

These employees are known in the workplace as aggressive, no-nonsense, and take-charge individuals. When they focus their energies properly, they can become overachievers and are extremely productive. They are often perceived by their peers as backstabbing employees who are constantly looking to get ahead at the expense of others.

When stress is added, these individuals struggle to regain control of their workplace environment by thrusting themselves in front of any peers who will listen. While they may have no confidential insight, they talk as though they do. They can be overheard explaining the direction the company is going in and why the company is going there. They throw out ideas and opinions at the watercooler, in the lunchroom, and anywhere else they can find an audience. They are disruptive at departmental meetings and are frequently heard criticizing management. As time passes, these individuals tend to become more aggressive and develop short-fused tempers.

In troubled times, companies perceive these employees as a threat to any successful turnaround because they challenge management's decisions and try to persuade their peers to agree with them. Managers dread working with these individuals because they are difficult to get along with and quickly become openly hostile.

Type B Personality Individuals

These are employees who present themselves as mild-mannered and possessing an even temperament. They typically are content to follow management's directions. They are well liked by their peers, trusted by management, and generally considered dependable but not flashy.

As stress is added during hard economic times, an employee with this demeanor skips lunch or eats at his or her desk. These employees never stray from their workstations because they think close proximity to their desks is a determining factor of who keeps their jobs. They stop interacting with their peers, and their productivity plummets. They avoid standing out, never volunteer, refuse to talk at meetings, and retreat as quickly as possible back to their workstations where they can disappear. Managers find these individuals frustrating to manage.

Personality Transformations

Employees are very perceptive about how the company is doing, particularly when it is struggling or going through an economic downturn. As an employee, you don't need to read a newspaper article or a press release to find out if the company is struggling. Often, the heightened stress level permeating throughout the company hallways is so thick that it can be sensed even by a visitor. The tension is so palpable and so suffocating that it is barely tolerable to be in the building. But, as an employee, there you are. And you need to be there every day.

With prolonged, heightened stress levels, you will quickly begin to see personality shifts in your peers. Their frustration and stress may manifest itself in different ways. Some become withdrawn and

29

quiet and attempt to disappear into the company masses. Others become vocal about their discontent with the company and talk openly about this. Still others will unwisely step up as know-it-all spokespersons for the company and falsely proclaim that they are "in the know" on what is occurring behind closed doors. The rarest employee is the one who does not experience a personality change and who stays focused on his or her job. The focused employee has the best chance of surviving the next round of job eliminations. Based on my experience, employees of this type are few and far between.

"Withdrawn" employees have an increased chance of losing their employment because of their visible and noticeable detachment from the job. Managers fear that withdrawn employees won't be able to rebound to their pre-stress productive selves and handle their job responsibilities. Managers believe, and rightfully so, that these employees will become even less productive after additional job eliminations are announced.

A "know-it-all" employee is the most dangerous type of employee to become or listen to. This employee type is frequently found holding spontaneous meetings with their peers. This employee tries to gain popularity by discussing fabricated inside information and knowledge of the company's plans. In reality, information pertaining to job eliminations is generally held in a small group of need-to-know members of management. Companies planning significant changes in staffing become painfully quiet before any announcements. Managers are advised by their legal counsel that confidentiality during the formative stages of the game plan is required to limit potential liability exposure. Human resources professionals also argue that confidentiality is required for successful implementation. The cone of silence that is placed on management during this time period is awkward for lower-level managers because they are the ones being barraged daily with questions from employees concerned about their jobs.

The quiet period fosters even more unrest with the workforce and provides a perfect environment for the know-it-all employees to step up and fill the void for peers desperately seeking information about the company's plans. Know-it-all employees become increasingly more believable when their comments are not met with a rebuttal from management. Rest assured that managers note those who step up as know-it-all employees and deal swiftly with them when the game plan is implemented. As a general rule, the know-it-all employees are on the next list of job eliminations because they are considered to be a threat to management.

"Discontented" employees are individuals who can't shield their emotions during the quiet period. They will outwardly behave in ways that draw management's attention. Their behavior cannot be tolerated and needs to be addressed immediately to avoid its spreading throughout the workplace. The emotional instability of discontented employees brought on by the heightened stress level may result in management pursuing disciplinary action based on performance issues, leading to termination prior to the announcement of job eliminations. Unfortunately, these employees will not have job elimination on their permanent records; instead, their records will bear the black mark of termination for cause. Additionally, they will not be able to count on the company for a good reference in the future.

"Focused" employees are seen as individuals who continue to be engaged with their jobs. They are company-oriented and flexible enough to change with the new developments at the company. The focused employee type will typically survive job cuts. However, if they want to heighten their job security, focused employees need to adapt their work strategy from working hard to working smart and subliminally convince their manager that they are indispensable to the manager's own job security.

One of the more important factors in the behavior of those who survive job eliminations is their support for the company's initiatives. In this context, support means they agree that the work can be restructured in such a way that it can be performed more efficiently by fewer employees. However, they must be careful not to beat the drum too loudly for the company, or they will lose the camaraderie of their peers.

In planning your strategy and implementing techniques to save your job, remember that you need to be perceived as believing and supporting the company game plan and business model. It is irrelevant whether you actually agree with it or not. The time to complain is at home and not at work. The time to pretend is at work and not at home. If you're viewed as not embracing the company business model, it becomes almost impossible for your manager to keep you if there is another round of job eliminations. You must avoid putting your manager in the situation where your retention can be construed as an alliance with a disgruntled employee.

Never participate in a discussion assessing whether the right people lost their jobs. This argument cannot be won and will be divisive toward either your peers or your manager. The decision has already been made and implemented, so move on.

Rule of Thumb
You don't have to like or be happy about what is occurring in your workplace. You just have to be cognizant of your personality and ensure that you are perceived by your manager as being happier than your peers.

CHAPTER 5

ZOMBIES ALWAYS DIE FIRST

A true but adapted story:

While participating in a meeting at a regional office of a newly acquired company, we adjourned to the lunchroom to watch a scheduled video conference held by the CEO of the acquiring Fortune 500 company. The conference was tailored to employees in the North American operations. After her brief introductory remarks, the CEO explained her vision of the structure of the blended companies. One particular slide revealed that the process engineering department of every facility would report to the Fortune 500 company's home office. According to the CEO, the decision was based on her desire to standardize operations across the North American sites.

The reason the CEO gave for the change in the reporting relationship of the process engineering departments meant nothing to the affected personnel. I am confident that no reason or justification would have pacified that group. After the meeting, I observed the group laughing about the ignorance of the CEO. They believed that no one could understand the facility's capabilities and problems from a remote location.

Shortly after the CEO's message, each facility had assigned corporate representatives working at the site seven days a week. This was the case for several months. Some of the facility personnel shunned the corporate representatives and were not forthcoming about the site, the status of ongoing projects, and the chronic problems at the location. Other facility personnel were blatantly obnoxious and kept referring the corporate representatives to the blueprints, implying that they should figure it out for themselves. These employees must have assumed that they would have job protection as long as the corporate representatives did not have a good understanding of the facility. Several employees at the facility who cooperated with the corporate representatives and commented on how they saw this as an exciting opportunity to finally bring shared "best practices" to their facility.

While it took close to nine months, the corporate representatives did acquire a clear understanding of the facility without the help of all the site personnel. The Fortune 500 company realized that the facility had many more mechanical issues than previously believed. The decision was made to transfer additional resources to the facility to finish outstanding construction work and permanently address the chronic problems. The facility personnel who stonewalled the corporate representatives were terminated because they could not be trusted. Cooperating facility personnel kept their jobs, and some were promoted to take the positions of those who were asked to leave.

***

Fear Is for Zombies

Whether you heard a rumor that job eliminations were coming, survived earlier job eliminations, or are just cognizant of the fact that the backlog of work has drastically declined, there are many reasons why you may become fearful for your job. Fear is a normal reaction, but in the workplace, it is not acceptable and must be concealed. Individuals who can't control their fear are commonly referred to in the human resources world as "the walking dead" or "zombies." As you probably guessed, these terms cast a disparaging light on the employees and are a stigma equivalent to wearing the scarlet letter. Therefore, if you let your fear control your actions, your fear of losing your job may become self-fulfilling.

Employees who fear losing their jobs often believe that they are safe if they keep a low profile until business improves. Maintaining a low profile can manifest itself in many ways, including absenteeism, avoidance of managers, and skipping social events after work such as a company volleyball game. While almost every employee will experience the "zombie" syndrome, it is how long you remain in this state that ultimately determines your job security. It is easy to tell when an employee is paralyzed with fear. If you are unable to control your fear or at least conceal it at work, your performance will suffer. Management interprets your fear in one of two ways: you have permanently lost interest in your job, or you cannot be relied on to pitch in when things get tough. Either way, you are obviously sending the wrong message. Remember, "zombies" are always eliminated.

Perception Is Your Manager's Reality

Many employees who are stricken with fear begin to search for a new job with a more stable company. The job search may become the focus of their attention. When this change in mindset occurs, it affects their personality. It also becomes abundantly clear to their peers and—more importantly—to their manager that they have emotionally quit their job.

If you choose to look for another job, you must resist any change to your mindset concerning your dedication to your present job. While the decision to look for another job might be in your best interests, you must be vigilant in ensuring that this decision does not unconsciously cause you to become a detached employee. Detached behavior has several signs similar to those shown by an individual in the "zombie" state, including an observable waning interest in the job. Additional signs of detachment are habitual tardiness, leaving work early, excessive telephone calls (particularly if they are cell phone calls), long lunches and breaks, management bashing, and absenteeism.

Whether you are paralyzed with fear or emotionally detached from your job, you must conceal these feelings. Your manager's perception of you as a "focused" employee who is still committed to the job must not change. Your observable actions and attitude need to be consistent and unwavering right through the time you leave your employer for a new job. Otherwise, you may find that you have created a situation where your name is moved to the top of the list for elimination before you are able to find a new job. This is not an enviable position.

Because many others are experiencing the same emotions as you, step up and take advantage of this opportunity by differentiating yourself from your peers. Look for ways to demonstrate to your manager that you are a go-to employee when things are tough. It is irrelevant whether it is true; it is only important that your manager believes it to be true. This provides you with job security while management begins the process of separating "zombies" from their jobs. Even if you plan on leaving, it is smart to become the go-to employee because it allows you to leave under your own time frame.

Rule of Thumb

To keep your job or to buy more time while looking for another, you must not allow your emotions to affect your behavior. By simply remaining consistent in your actions and behavior, you will be perceived as a focused, go-to employee. In addition, you will stand out thanks to the behavior of your peers, which will undoubtedly deteriorate.

CHAPTER 6

START COLLECTING HATS

More than likely, the work that you perform and the methods of completing the same differ from the job description for your position. This is a common situation, and from the viewpoint of the employees, it is really of no significance. The ever changing world and the need for companies to react quickly to global market demands, customer expectations, and financial pressures necessitates, to a certain extent, that companies and their workforces be flexible. Companies that lack the ability to work in a fluid environment and that attempt to establish overly exhaustive black-and-white guidelines and rigid job descriptions for their employees often struggle to survive.

A History Lesson about Job Descriptions

While attorneys strongly encourage companies to institute up-to-date job descriptions for its employees, companies still fail to do so for several reasons. One reason is that companies cannot justify budgeting such an extensive amount of resources to a task that will end with a product that is outdated the day it is completed. Job descriptions are labor intensive and require an extensive amount of hours from both managers and the employees whose jobs are being reviewed. Companies get around the federal and state law requirements by simply adding broad language, which was developed by legal counsel, to their job descriptions. Specifically, companies add a catchall statement to their job descriptions that stipulates "that employees are responsible for all other duties as assigned." Basically, the company can then ask you to perform just about any work-related task, and it falls within your job description.

Job Eliminations Start with Job Descriptions

Because the courts have held that the broad language in job descriptions is valid in many different contexts, companies are reluctant to set aside valuable resources to maintain job descriptions in their specifics. You would expect this to be particularly true in an economic downturn when companies are scrutinizing every dollar spent. However, this generally is not the case for reasons different than you might guess.

You might be wondering right now why your company recently asked you to complete a job description form for your position. The form probably requested that you detail what you do and the amount of time you spend on each component of your job. I am confident in my assertion that struggling companies do not spend time and money to perform this type of administrative housekeeping just to keep their attorneys content. Despite what you were told, the purpose of updating your job description was more than likely to capture your job responsibilities in better detail. This information will help senior management, human resources personnel, and the corporate attorney understand how your role actually corresponds to the end product. The updated job description is critical in figuring out if the work can be performed differently and with fewer employees. It also will be used to structure job eliminations in a legally defendable manner.

Wearing Many Hats May Be the Key

Smart companies get a clear understanding of how work is actually performed before redesigning workflows. When companies redesign their workflow, they see their workforce as bloated and ripe for reduction. Managers are instructed to sift through their direct reports and identify those who can be successful under the new design. The employees who are most likely to survive are those who have broad backgrounds and are viewed as utility players. These employees have demonstrated in the past that they have the ability to help out wherever and whenever needed by the company and their manager. Ironically, employees who were considered excellent workers in the past may no longer be viewed favorably under the new workflow. Because job responsibilities are about to change, past efficiency and productivity on specific, narrow tasks no longer carry much weight. Basically, employees who have demonstrated the ability to "wear many hats" are perceived as more likely to be able to adapt to change and succeed in the new, redesigned environment.

Rule of Thumb
When work flows are being modified because of job eliminations, companies view employees who are adaptable to change and have diversified work experiences as more valuable than those with specific specialties. Remember, if you want to save your job, broader is better when it comes to experience.

CHAPTER 7

ANY VOLUNTEERS?

Managers are trained to identify employees for job elimination based on work-related criteria. The fact remains, however, that a manager's personal relationship with an employee skews objectivity in favor of that employee. If you exploit the various opportunities set forth in this book, this lack of objectivity can work in your favor and result in your name being left off of or stricken from the list of employees who will lose their jobs.

Volunteer for Yourself

In times of crisis, every employee has to grab a fire extinguisher and help put out the unexpected daily fires that arise. They need to do this while simultaneously performing their regular job responsibilities and project work. Along with the upheaval, the economic turmoil will cause your company to have an abundance of opportunities for you to demonstrate your abilities. Many employees mistakenly refuse to volunteer for additional assignments or project work when the company cannot promise a future reward. Their mistake provides you with an opportunity to exploit and capitalize on. By volunteering for assignments, you are primarily looking out for yourself by acquiring new talents that can be listed on your résumé. You may never have the chance again to get paid while you develop new skills.

As a bonus, your manager will welcome your eagerness to help out. It makes your manager's life easier, increases your worth to your manager, and ultimately increases the likelihood of keeping your job. Your best chance of staying employed in a tight economy is for you to be perceived as a focused go-to employee who can help your manager stay employed. The fact that you are looking for ways to build your résumé for your next company should you be let go is our little secret.

Tips, Please!

Because managers often seek out volunteers for project work

prior to assigning personnel to the project, this is a slow pitch of an opportunity that you should be prepared to knock out of the park. There are guidelines that need to be considered in identifying a hidden gem mixed in with the available project work. If selected properly, the next project you volunteer for can help you control your destiny in the workplace. If you merely volunteer for a project haphazardly, you may inadvertently move yourself one step closer to unemployment. Project work can come in many shapes and forms, but it can basically be categorized into three groups:

- long- or short-term projects
- individual or team projects
- intradepartmental or interdepartmental projects

Long- or Short-Term Projects?

Regardless of whether job eliminations are occurring in companies throughout the country or just in your company, survival techniques are required. Project work, if viewed properly and utilized strategically, can provide you with a lifeline that saves your job. Short-term projects are an excellent method to showcase your talents quickly, but they are fraught with potential pitfalls that can easily result in your early dismissal. Before volunteering for a short-term project, consider the probability of accomplishing the project before the essential variables change. In particular, consider how long the project will realistically take and whether it can be completed prior to the company cutting the budget hours and funding. You must avoid projects that have an unrealistic time frame. These projects invariably have their resources diverted away prior to completion, leaving you and your name permanently affixed to a failed project.

Unlike short-term projects that allow you to showcase your knowledge, skills, and abilities quickly, the benefit of a long-term project is that it provides a safe haven if the project is considered by management to be significant to the overall success of the company. Managers are less likely to identify employees for job elimination when they are assigned to long-term projects. Managers who do so place their own jobs at risk should the project subsequently fail because of the disruption. No manager is willing to guarantee the success of the project at the cost of their own job.

Individual or Team Projects?
When vying for assignments, you need to determine if it will be an individual or a team project prior to volunteering. Individual project work is a great means to stand out in the workplace when successful. On the flip side, you walked yourself to the guillotine if the project fails. Only select an individual project if you are extremely confident that you have the competence, budget, and time to finish the project. Individual projects need to be short-term goal-oriented to ensure that you can complete them before further deterioration in the economy or the company. Things change rapidly in an economic downturn, and deterioration can result in the budgeted amount of time or money for your project vanishing. Trust me, it does not matter if the project fails solely because of budget cutbacks, you will be remembered as the employee who worked on a failing project that wasted the company's money. Your manager will also be tagged with overseeing a failed project. This is not the supportive message that you hope to get across to your manager in troubled times.

Team projects have several interesting dynamics associated with them. If the project fails, regardless of the reason, you have some security being in a group and not standing alone to take the fall. Additionally, working in a group allows you to stay connected to the grapevine and hear more information about company developments than if you work alone. Be careful, however, to differentiate fact from rumors that often circulate in distressed companies. Another benefit to volunteering for a team project is that when it is successfully completed, you gain recognition, albeit in a lesser amount than if you performed an individual project.

Intradepartmental or Interdepartmental?
Projects that require interdepartmental staffing are to be preferred over those requiring intradepartmental staffing. Interdepartmental projects allow you to meet new peers and managers within the company and broaden your network of contacts. By definition, interdepartmental projects cut across departmental lines and therefore provide you with broader experiences that can be added to your résumé. As discussed later in this book, you need to plan for the worst while hoping for the best in difficult economic times. Continue to update and strengthen your résumé by volunteering for project work that will provide you with new experiences. Simultaneously, distinguish yourself as a focused employee who

can be considered a go-to employee by your manager. After all, every manager appreciates a direct report who volunteers for project work. Additionally, volunteering for interdepartmental project work increases your network of contacts. This will be invaluable to you should your job be eliminated. The more work peers you can contact when you're out of work, the better your chances of finding a new job.

In difficult times, companies seek to cut costs. Reducing headcount, though shortsighted, is one of the quickest ways to improve the bottom line. Employees who keep their jobs tend to have broader experiences and have demonstrated their ability to wear more hats. By broadening your exposure to new experiences, or at least demonstrating your willingness to do so, you raise your value to your manager and increase the likelihood of staying employed.

Rule of Thumb
Look for ways to broaden your skill set and showcase your experience through strategically selected volunteer projects. Volunteer project work that cuts across departmental lines can widen your networking circle and should be preferred if all else is equal.

CHAPTER 8

SCREW THE COMPANY GOALS

As quickly as the financial health of companies change during an economic downturn, so do company priorities. Companies shift their scarce resources, including manpower, funding, and supplies, to a scaled-down number of priorities that are viewed as critical to the company's survival. Managers are pressured from company leaders to improve profit margins immediately through elimination of departmental inefficiencies. The first place managers look to tighten their belts and streamline operations is headcount. With your company and manager changing priorities from long-term growth to short-term survival, it is time for you to also reevaluate your action items and revisit your priorities.

Your manager can easily get overwhelmed with the changing business demands being placed on the department and the micromanagement of departmental issues. It is incumbent upon you to step forward and ask your manager to reconsider the specific priorities that were previously set for you. For self-serving reasons, your priorities should be reevaluated in collaboration with your manager. There is no reason to invest your efforts into an action item or previously set priority that will reap no reward for you and your manager. Don't waste your skills and the limited company resources on an outdated priority that will go unnoticed even if you are successful beyond your wildest imagination.

Because long-term company goals may not be perfectly aligned with your manager's short-term goal of remaining employed, a review of priorities is always prudent. Managers make a self-serving assessment of what priorities or projects will make them look valuable to the company's leaders. A manager will quickly abandon a long-term goal of the company in favor of a short-term victory that is beneficial to his or her status as a productive manager. Without stating the real reasons, managers often shift priorities that focus their employees' time to goals that will help the managers look better in the eyes of senior management. During economic

43

turmoil, even the most dedicated company manager will view every decision according to how it reflects on them from a self-preservation perspective.

When your priorities are realigned, you will be given action items that improve your manager's chance of surviving the next round of job eliminations and do not necessarily reflect what is in the company's best interests. Managers also tend to shift resources to those employees performing work that make the manager's life easier. This should be perfectly acceptable to you. Remember, your manager's goals are your goals as well. Your best chance of staying employed is to assist your manager in staying employed. Nothing should be considered more important than making your manager feel a debt of gratitude toward you. After all, your manager will be responsible for making the selection of which individuals will be eliminated. Accomplishing a company goal is insignificant if it does not result in the improvement of your manager's work life or job security.

When reestablishing priorities, you need to make sure that your manager budgets the appropriate resources for you. If not, explain your concerns immediately to your manager. You do not want to catch your manager off guard when a priority or project is not completed on time or within budget. In a bad economy, such a surprise to your manager will most assuredly result in your job elimination.

Rule of Thumb
Your manager's goals should be identical to yours at all times. In tough times, do not assume that the previously set company goals are the same as your manager's goal of survival in the workplace. Regroup with your manager, and refocus your efforts to demonstrate that you are a valuable resource to your manager's goal of staying employed.

CHAPTER 9

I WAS THERE

A true but adapted story:

Working for a progressive start-up company that grew every year by double digits through breakthrough advancements in its products, I marveled at how much the company promoted and valued open communication. To further open communication, human resources personnel persuaded the CEO that senior managers should be required to periodically eat in the general lunchroom individually and mingle with the company employees. The company additionally did away with assigned parking and initiated an annual employee appreciation day picnic where senior management barbecued the food themselves and served the employees.

The CEO was a quiet individual who truly deserved the label "workaholic." He arrived at work well before sunrise every morning. As far as I was concerned, there was no beating the CEO to work; well, at least I wasn't going to try. Turning into the company's unreserved parking lot each morning, I would see the CEO's car parked in the first row second spot. Who owned the first car meant nothing to me because I was always fixated on the second car, which riddled me with guilt as though I were arriving late.

I was working closely with senior management on a planned reduction of copy room staff and security personnel whose jobs became redundant with the modernization of equipment and the installation of security cameras. The copy room personnel were going to decrease from twenty-five to eight, and the number of security guards was going to decrease from twelve to three. As usual, a week before the rollout and announcement of the job eliminations, the plans were shared with the CEO for the first time. The cost savings associated with the plan spoke for itself. The meeting lasted only several minutes and ended abruptly when the pressed-for-time CEO shook his head to acknowledge approval, arose from the conference table, and returned to his desk. While two members of senior management and I were exiting through the rich mahogany executive doors, the CEO uttered his only comment on the plan. "Just make sure my coffee buddy keeps his job. He has a sick mother-in-law who lives with him," the CEO stated.

As it turned out, his coffee buddy was the overnight security guard. We later learned that the security guard walked through the executive suite each morning while performing his final security check before turning the security detail over to the day shift. Coffee buddy owned the car parked in the first parking spot. Over the years, a simple friendship formed between the CEO and the security guard in the silence of an empty office building before the break of dawn. Unbeknownst to anyone, the CEO would chat for a few minutes each morning with the security guard over a cup of coffee. These simple chats saved that security guard's job. He was removed from the list of individuals to be eliminated. After all, "coffee buddy" had a sick mother-in-law living with him.

***

Arrive Early or Stay Late?

For those of you who try to impress your manager with your dedication to the job by working late, I have bad news for you. Managers do not buy this tactic. They assume that you leave immediately after them, particularly in situations where your work product is not immediately tangible. Working closely with managers over several decades, I am confident that managers almost universally share this perception. While I agree with the concept that working longer hours is a smart move to show your dedication when layoffs are abundant, it has to be done correctly. For starters, to ensure that your extra efforts are noticed, get to work before your manager arrives.

There is another reason that arriving early for work has a better result than staying late. Arriving before your manager significantly increases the chances that your manager will ask what you're working on that has you coming in so early. This conversation is almost certain to occur as early as the second day of your coming in early. Working late, on the other hand, very seldom prompts a discussion with your manager, even if it is noticed. By the time the next day rolls around, your working late is old news, and your manager's attention is focused on the new problems that need to be addressed. In difficult economic times, there is always a new problem rearing its ugly head. While this advice may seem oversimplified, it is practical and time-tested. If you're going to work longer hours to impress your manager, you must make the necessary adjustment to your strategy to ensure that you receive the positive, predictable outcome of having your extra efforts noticed.

There are other methods of maximizing the chances of your manager noticing your extra efforts. You can increase your chances of being noticed by parking where your manager typically parks, passing by your manager's office first thing in the morning, or sending an e-mail to your manager outside of normal working hours. In doing this, you need to keep your credibility intact. This is easily achieved as long as you have a valid reason for passing by your manager's office or for sending the e-mail. If need be, hold off on a substantive e-mail you were going to send the day before, and send it when you arrive early the next day. Even if you drafted the e-mail already, if there is no immediate deadline, save it and send it the following morning. The time stamp on the e-mail speaks for itself. If the e-mail is substantive, your manager will assume that you were there for an extended period of time prior to the time stamp. This way you get credit for your extra efforts without having to say a word. Well-timed e-mails are an excellent method of demonstrating your willingness to work hard to ease your manager's burden without being too gratuitous about it.

Rule of Thumb

By ensuring that your efforts are noticed by your manager, you will be perceived as a "focused" employee and thereby increase your chances of staying employed.

CHAPTER 10

NEVER TRAVEL ALONE

A true but adapted story:

While preparing to write about this chapter, I recalled one of the cruelest job eliminations that I ever participated in. I was involved in the activity leading up to and including the decision to eliminate the Chief Information Officer (CIO), but I was not the bearer of bad news in this case. My presence was required merely to oversee how the discussion played out.

Corporate attorneys and human resources professionals agree that it is a bad practice to inform an employee of a job elimination when that employee is out of the office or traveling. It allows too much room for the situation and discussion to deteriorate—both of which the manager needs to control. The preferred technique is to talk to the affected employee at the place of employment.

In the situation here, the CIO was overseeing the implementation of a new global networking platform. The rollout and conversion required extensive travel on her part. During the implementation, the CEO grew frustrated with cost overruns and the constant complaints received from operations personnel about how long the conversion was taking. The CEO determined that the CIO had placed the company in unnecessary jeopardy through mistakes in budgeting time and money and that she needed to be replaced.

After a new CIO was found, the CEO became impatient about bringing the new CIO onboard. On a Friday afternoon, the CEO had his assistant schedule a video conference meeting with the information technology department personnel for the next Monday so that he could announce the new CIO. A wrinkle arose when the CEO received a telephone call from the current CIO on Monday morning. The CIO stated that her family met her in Florida over the weekend and that she decided to take a couple days off to spend time with her children at Walt Disney World.

Disregarding my advice and the pleas of human resources personnel, the CEO decided to go ahead with the announcement meeting. The CEO called the present CIO's cell phone shortly before the video conference. I was asked to sit in on the conference call. The CIO learned of her job elimination while standing in line with her children for an attraction at Walt Disney World. To this day, I still shake my head about how inappropriately that news was delivered.

***

Is Travel Consistent with Your Manager's Goals?

During times of unrest at the workplace, many employees seek the comfort and solitude of business travel. They mistakenly believe that management will view their business travel as dedication to the job. They convince themselves that they will be perceived as an employee who is focused on the task at hand amidst the turbulent waters of the business. In reality, the employee seeks to hide from the stress of the workplace in much the same way that the "zombies" do back at the office. Even if you successfully convince your manager that travel is required, travel at this trying time is a costly mistake in judgment.

To improve your chances of saving your job, you need to become a go-to employee for your manager. This requires a heightened level of visibility. During troubled times, your manager experiences stress comparable to yours and will seek to find someone to share the increased burdens with. Managers look for subordinates who can help them. If you're not around, they will find a coworker who is. Let's put this into context: while you're traveling to help the company, your coworker is at the office helping your manager. As previously noted, your manager's goals are often separate and distinct from those of the company during an economic downturn. Your manager's goal of remaining employed and the priorities that support that goal should be your only concern. The difference between pleasing your manager or the company is monumental when your manager has to make decisions regarding which employees will keep their jobs and which will be eliminated.

When Is Travel Encouraged?

Situations change rapidly in the business world during economic downturns. If traveling is required, then by all means go. Be objective in determining the validity of the travel to make sure that you are not sinking into the zombie syndrome. However, if you do travel, you need to stay connected to the office and to your manager. With improved technology, communication is easy and never far from your fingertips. Check in frequently with the office to determine if there are any developments. You need to ensure that your manager understands that you are an available resource despite traveling. If there is a company announcement, you should contact your manager and inquire as to how it will impact his or her position. Remember to ask if there is anything you can do.

On the flip side, travel with your manager is always a great opportunity. Travel provides a perfect setting for you to get to know your manager on a different level over an extended period of time. It allows you to gain insight into what is occurring in your manager's world in a depressurized situation. The more you understand your manager's issues, the easier it is for you to assist your manager. This gives you a significant competitive advantage over your peers. It provides you with insight on how to best support your manager and be perceived as a go-to employee. As you may recall, your goal is to make your manager's life easier and perhaps keep your manager employed. This, in turn, will give you an advantage when your manager begins deciding which employees to let go.

Rule of Thumb
While your peers mistakenly attempt to get out of harm's way by avoiding management through travel, going out for lunch, or hiding in their offices or cubicles, you need to step up and fill the void by becoming more visible and supportive of your manager.

CHAPTER 11

BIG BROTHER IS WATCHING

With the modernization of communication methods, employees are able to perform their jobs more efficiently and from remote locations. These same technology advancements allow companies to closely monitor the time and whereabouts of their employees. It is amazing that employees still foolishly think that they will not get caught using company technology for their own personal use. For decades, companies have been terminating employees for improper or unauthorized use of computers, telephones, cell phones, scanners, and fax machines. The most recent and probably the most intrusive method companies are presently using to track their employees is the global positioning system (GPS). Without a doubt, this technology is the modern-day Achilles' heel for employees.

You're on Notice

Any self-respecting company has its employees sign an acknowledgement that they will not use company-provided equipment for matters other than company business. In furtherance of the acknowledgement, the employee handbook usually states that the company has the right to monitor the usage of any company-owned equipment. If the company determines that an employee is using the company technology for matters other than company business, the employee is typically disciplined up to and including termination of employment.

Why do employees still check job opportunity Web sites on computers provided by the company? Some employees do so out of pure stupidity, while others do so out of arrogance over their ability to hide their Web site navigation trail. Still others are ignorant of how companies monitor their technology and think that they can only get caught if they are seen by management or are selected for a random audit by human resources. Below, I discuss the most common reasons I have heard for misusing company computers and explain the inaccuracies of the employee's thinking.

- Employee Reason Number 1: My manager was never round, so I didn't think I had to worry.

Inaccuracy Explanation: The manager frequently has nothing to do with an employee getting caught. The company's information technology department captures and stores data on where employees visit on the Web. This information is used to create reports that are prepared for and shared with the company's managers.

- Employee Reason Number 2: With all the employees in the company, why would anyone check my computer usage as long as my manager is content?

Inaccuracy Explanation: Every company has the capability, whether it uses it or not, to set up monitoring software that prepares reports at specified intervals detailing what employees are doing on their computers. While it seems to be common knowledge among employees that companies capture information when an employee goes to an adult Web site, employees are ignorant of the fact that companies also monitor which employees go to job posting Web sites (i.e., Monster.com, CareerBuilder.com). The information technology department typically disseminates reports containing this information to the managers of employees appearing in the reports every week regardless if requested by the manager. Do not interpret your manager's silence on the matter as lack of knowledge or your success in going undetected. There are many reasons why a manager may not address the issue immediately. One such reason is that the employee has made the manager's job easier by basically volunteering to be an employee who will be eliminated in the next wave of layoffs.

- Employee Reason Number 3: Sure it was the company's laptop, but it was after hours while traveling.

Inaccuracy Explanation: Companies do not differentiate between working and nonworking hours when you are using their equipment.

- Employee Reason Number 4: My computer at home was broken.

Inaccuracy Explanation: So what? Stop at the library to use a free computer on the way home. This is a personal favorite of mine in the sense that I truly believe these employees deserve what they get if they are that lazy.

How Can You Abuse a GPS?

For the most part, employees understand that companies are serious when they state that they monitor their technology. For some reason, though, employees do not view the global positioning system with the same deference. They need to wake up and realize that the global positioning system technology is every bit as telling of an employee's actions as any other company technology assigned to them. Navigation systems provide exact location of the device at specific times. While it helps employees who travel or make deliveries perform their jobs, it also helps companies monitor the whereabouts of their employees.

Through navigation system tracking, outside salespeople have been caught taking frolics of their own (side trips) on their way to scheduled meetings. Managers have been found to be going home for extended periods of time when they were supposedly monitoring outside projects. Company cars have been discovered traveling out of state for personal vacations. This list could continue, but the point has been achieved.

Companies looking to eliminate jobs have much more data in their possession than employees like to think or believe. Be smart, and expect that all technology provided by the company is actively monitored. Assume that all personal use of company property is captured and will be used against you at such time as the company decides that it needs to reduce employee headcount. Control your destiny by behaving in a professional manner when using company technology. This is one of the easiest ways to keep your name off the list of those who will have their jobs eliminated.

Rule of Thumb
Be smart, and don't move yourself to the top of the list of employees who will undergo job elimination. Act in a responsible and professional manner when using company technology, and refrain from any personal use of such equipment.

CHAPTER 12

FORCE THE CASUAL MEETING

With more and more companies heeding the advice of human resources professionals, it is more common than ever before for CEOs and other senior management members to attempt to send the message that no company employee is more valuable than another. Many CEOs adhere to this philosophy and look for informal communication methods (i.e., subliminal) to demonstrate this and hopefully improve morale in the workforce. A technique commonly used by companies to communicate this message is requiring the executives and managers to use the general company parking lot and the general lunchroom. If your company subscribes to this thinking, do not let this opportunity escape you. If exploited correctly, it can improve your chances of controlling your destiny in the workplace.

Opportunity Is Knocking

There are a variety of ways to exploit this opportunity depending upon where the situation arises. Although the opportunity can occur in an endless number of locations, such as the parking lot, lunchroom, company picnic, or holiday party, I will discuss the parking lot scenario in this chapter. The forethought discussed below in preparing for the forced casual meeting is the same regardless of where it takes place.

Start by noting where the key managers for your career will be at a given time. (For the parking lot example, note where they park their car and the time they arrive.) Key managers will include your immediate manager but should also encompass managers in areas that you would like to cross into perhaps through an interdepartmental project. Because people are creatures of habit and tend to have daily routines, it should be relatively easy to determine where they park their cars or sit in the lunchroom every day. Besides, after a member of management parks in the same spot for several consecutive days, the parking spot is marked the same as when an animal in the wild marks its territory. No one dares intrude by taking that space without permission.

Script the Conversation in Advance

Before you engage a key manager for your career in a forced casual meeting, you need to think about what you will say. You need to be in the driver's seat when it comes to the flow of the conversation. Determine in advance what you want to accomplish. Next, plan on what you will say and what you will ask to accomplish this goal. This may sound like common sense or even overkill. However, many people stumble into a forced causal meeting with no game plan and end up coming across as pushy and overly aggressive. Leaving a key manager with a bad first impression of you completely undermines your plan of increasing your chances of surviving the next wave of job eliminations. Because forced encounters are brief in nature and last a few minutes at most, you need to develop an approach that gets information across but at a controlled pace over several meetings.

In preparing for the forced casual meeting, you should create a short elevator speech. An elevator speech is nothing more than a concise statement that explains who you are, what you have accomplished and where you would like your career to go. In my opinion, a great elevator speech lasts between thirty to forty-five seconds. If you speak uninterrupted for more than forty-five seconds, the listener has probably tuned you out. Moreover, the listener may find you pompous, conceited, or boring and avoid you in the future. The purpose of the elevator speech is to pique the interest of the listener and prompt questions from the listener. Most everyone can identify when an elevator speech has been thrown at them. Some individuals are insulted with the template approach. Therefore, while appropriate for use on people outside of the company, you should never use a prepared elevator speech on a key manager at your present company.

The preparation of an elevator speech is nonetheless useful. It is a great tool to force you to think about your career from both a hindsight and a foresight perspective. For many people, especially those who have been with the same company for an extended period of time, this exercise may be the first time they reflected on their career since they created a résumé to land their present job years ago. The elevator speech additionally requires you to hone your skills in self-promoting yourself in a succinct manner. Many times, thoughts about the highlights of your career and where you would like to see your career go may come quickly to you. However, plans for how to best present that information in such a short time frame seldom comes as quickly.

The forced casual meeting is not the time to persuade someone of your brilliance or your importance to the company. It is the time to start to develop a personal connection between yourself and someone who can potentially help you down the road with your career or even save your job. When initiating a forced casual meeting with a key manager outside of your chain of command, tread carefully. The personal connection needs to be cultivated over many meetings. You need to start very casually and achieve your primary goal of identifying yourself by name, department, and position within the company. The basic information about you that I just noted is also the same information that appears on the sheet listing the employees who are to be eliminated. Key decision makers look over the names of employees being eliminated prior to the rollout of the job eliminations. Familiarity with a name on the list has often resulted in a call from a key decision maker that saves the familiar person's job.

Your accomplishments, experience, and goals should not be mentioned at the first meeting or any successive meeting with a key manager of your present company unless the key manager asks questions that undoubtedly take the conversation in that direction. Likewise, no discussion should ever be brought up about your job security. The implication that you are seeking a favor from the key manager (i.e., job protection) will undoubtedly result in a trust issue that prevents you from ever gaining the benefit of the forced casual meeting.

A forced casual meeting with your company manager typically evolves quicker. You may want to talk more openly about your goals, but once again, do not do this unless your manager takes the discussion there with questions. Even with your company manager, if you are too aggressive, your efforts can easily backfire as self-serving promotion. The results of such a mistake are that you lose credibility and torpedo your plan to improve your chances of being perceived as someone the manager can rely on.

Avoid Emotionally Charged Topics

A forced casual meeting needs to be light and airy when you are controlling the conversation or asking questions. Avoid discussions about emotionally charged topics such as politics, religion, or the like. If the key manager is your company manager, you should additionally refrain from work-related topics if possible when you're not in the work environment. The forced casual meeting is the time and place for you to start a personal dialogue with a key manager or your company manager. By keeping the conversation out of the work context and shifting it to a more personal level, you get the most benefit from the meeting.

Implement the Plan

Now that you have identified the key managers for your career, determined where they park their cars, and scripted the conversation, it is time to force the casual meeting. Arrive early enough to work to ensure that you can park near one of the key managers. Preferably, you can park immediately next to a key manager. Parking next to a key manager has many perks. It allows you to meet a manager that may be out of your daily work circle of contacts. The informal setting of the parking lot promotes open and casual discussion regardless of your rank in the company hierarchy. If you use these forced casual meetings properly, they can—over a period of time— create a relationship stronger than those you have with peers with whom you have worked for years.

Rule of Thumb

If planned in advance and exploited properly, the forced casual meeting is comparable to bumping into a key manager in your career at a social party. Knowing a key manager on even the slightest personal basis has resulted in continued employment for individuals who otherwise were to be terminated.

CHAPTER 13

TAKING ATTENDANCE

Employees are continuously bombarded with reminders of the dire straits of the economy. The harsh reality and pessimistic predictions on the economy can be found in every media form, including newspapers, television, Internet, and radio talk shows. Closer to home, employees read formal company press releases acknowledging that the company will not meet its predicted forecasts because demand for the company's products or services has fallen. Informally, but just as reliable, they learn at work that a large customer went out of business; they observe that the production line has slowed; they know that the company's back order of sales has dwindled; and they are fully cognizant that overtime is no longer offered. Employees do not need to be privy to confidential information in the senior management suites to realize that demand for their products or services must quickly improve or the company will start to eliminate jobs.

As the economy swirls in an economic whirlpool that threatens to pull every company and employee under, the mental health of the employees in the workplace plummets. The increased workplace stress experienced by employees can result in many undesirable but predictable outcomes. The first observable result of the heightened stress level is an increase in employee absenteeism. Prolonged tension in the workplace often leads to more severe problems, including higher incidences of harassment, physical intimidation, violence, and insubordination. The erratic behavior mentioned above may result in the human resources personnel requiring more employees than ever to submit to drug and alcohol screening based on reasonable suspicion of substance abuse on the job.

Coping with the heightened stress level becomes increasingly more difficult for employees as time goes on without improvement in the economy and the financial stability of their company. Even employees with companies that appear to be flourishing are not exempt from the stress. These employees live in a surreal world where their individual company appears to be immune to the economic downturn. Employees in these well-off companies often believe that their fate is much closer than it appears. Convinced that the company's good health is nothing more than the work of the public relations spin doctors, these employees often suffer similar stress levels. They live in fear every day that the company is concealing the truth about its condition. Their concern is not unfounded, taking into account the sensational news stories of companies that virtually collapsed overnight (i.e., Enron, Tyco, WorldCom).

Employees who are worn down emotionally and physically from workplace stress frequently take time off of work. Employees refer to these absences as "mental health days." They need a break from the workplace nonsense and time off to recharge their drained "emotional battery." Physicians are quick to accommodate an employee's request for a medical note, if required by the company, excusing the employee from work in such situations.

If I Need a Break, I'll Take a Break

Attendance is never more critical to saving your job than when the economy or, more importantly, your company is struggling through an economic downturn. Prior to making any headcount reduction decisions, companies routinely gather information that demonstrates the performance of their employees. One way they do this is by running numerous computer-generated reports about their employees. The first report they usually review is an attendance report. This allows for a quick side-by-side comparison of you and all your peers. This report is objective and does not separate who is a top performer and who is a slacker. This report simply favors employees who report to work each day regardless of the quality of their work and their productivity levels.

Attendance reports are run by date and are often used by companies to reveal which employees were most frequently absent during specific periods of time. Companies often assess which employees missed the most time after the last company layoff announcement. Employees taking time off after a layoff announcement are viewed with a high degree of suspicion. They are seen as employees who are disgruntled and who no longer enjoy coming to work. They are assumed to be job hunting. Even worse, they are assumed to be employees who are unable to embrace workplace change.

Companies believe that the employees who take time off shortly after a layoff announcement are in effect protesting the company's decision. Managers foolishly think that the employees remaining after the layoff should embrace the streamlining of the workforce because it allows these employees an opportunity to showcase their skills. With that viewpoint in mind, you understand why you must resist the temptation to take a "mental health day."

Hypocrisy at Its Worst

Absenteeism is perceived as a window into the mindset of the employee. Employees taking time off of work in troubled times are perceived as not being team players. Such employees are considered unwilling to help out when the company needs them most. In the eyes of the company, a dedicated employee makes it to work regardless of personal health or issues at home. The hypocrisy of this view is repulsive when you compare the terms and conditions of the average employee to those of senior managers.

Senior managers are entitled to more paid time off of work than average employees, attend company-paid management retreats during workdays to reinvigorate themselves, and have a more flexible schedule to attend to personal needs that occur during the day. However, this book is not about the equality of treatment in the workforce in the United States. If five decades of federal and state laws have not been able to accomplish that goal to date, I'm not so pompous to think that I can do it with this book. My purpose here is dedicated solely to helping you avoid me, the hatchet man.

You don't want to be on the top of an absentee list regardless of how the company is sorting information. Absenteeism is viewed as an employee who abuses the system. Sure the employee handbook states that it is a benefit, but in reality, that only applies when the economy is solid and the business is prosperous. Remember, your goal is for your manager to regard you as a go-to employee and someone who can be depended on. If your name appears on the absentee list, this may result in your manager thinking twice about your dependability. Even if your manager does view you as loyal to him or her, it requires him or her to openly justify his or her reasons for keeping you in subjective terms rather than objective terms. Do not put your manager in the situation where extra work is required to keep your name off the job elimination list. The underlying theme of this book is to improve your chances of remaining employed by making your manager's life easier. Creating extra work for your manager flies in the face of this premise and your goal.

Rule of Thumb

Like selfish children, managers expect total loyalty from their employees and think about nobody but themselves. Like a patient parent, play into your manager's selfishness but for your own self-serving reasons.

CHAPTER 14

DEBUNKING MYTHS

There are several myths circulating in the workplace about how employees can protect their jobs during a recession. These myths stem from federal and state laws that prohibit a company from retaliating against an employee who files a claim under certain laws, including those involving workers' compensation, harassment, or discrimination. While there are other rights that equally protect employees, these are the most prevalent and most commonly used by employees. Terminating an employee, of course, is considered retaliation and is therefore prohibited by law.

The myths are built on the assumption that if an employee strikes first, then the company cannot eliminate his or her job. Specifically, if the employee files a complaint with the company or an outside agency prior to the layoff announcement, the company is handcuffed and cannot eliminate his or her job. Like most myths, there are some elements of truth surrounding them, but they are exaggerated to the point that they reach an unrealistic conclusion. In this chapter, I will briefly discuss how the myths are thought to play out and if the myths are correct.

Filing a Work-Related Injury Report

Employees who file a workers' compensation claim with the appropriate state agency or report a work-related injury to the company are protected from retaliation for reporting the incident. State laws prohibiting retaliation ensure that there are no detrimental changes to the terms of that individual's employment, including termination resulting from the exercise of the employee's right to file the report.

This is by far the most common claim filed by unscrupulous or desperate employees seeking to stay on the company's payroll. In situations where news of a planned reduction in workforce leaks out prior to its implementation, these claims are filed in droves. They tend to be for injuries that are difficult for a company to medically disprove. Injuries that fall into this category are soft tissue injuries and sprains to the back or neck. Companies take these claims seriously and often conduct extensive investigations into the merits of these claims because they negatively impact the company's experience rating and raise its insurance premiums. As a word of caution, workers' compensation insurance providers occasionally turn a claim over to the local state's attorney for a criminal investigation if the claim looks suspicious. The criminal investigation is to determine if insurance fraud was committed.

Filing a Harassment or Discrimination Claim

Employees may file a discrimination or harassment claim for the same reason as those who file a work-related injury report: to ensure pay continuation and to prevent job termination. As mentioned above, federal and state laws prohibit companies from retaliating against employees who exercise their legal rights to file claims of harassment or discrimination in the workplace. Often, when word of an upcoming layoff announcement is spreading, employees file disingenuous claims with the human resources department or an outside agency prior to the actual announcement. Other employees prepare and wait to disclose to the company for the first time during the termination meeting that they were supposedly discriminated against or harassed. Federal and state laws are clear that employee's have the right to be free of harassment and discrimination in the workplace. The employee may allege that the harassment or discrimination was based on their race, color, national origin, sex, age, religion, disability, sexual orientation, or any other protected category. The employee may complain that a peer, a manager, or any other individual that he or she came in contact with during employment engaged in the unlawful activity. Again, companies take these claims seriously and investigate these matters thoroughly.

Real-World Outcomes

Now that you know how employees try to invoke the protections surrounding the myths, I will explain the reality of what occurs after the claim is filed. While this strategy may have worked at one time, companies and their attorneys are fully aware of and are prepared to defend against this job protection technique. Companies will not stand idly by while you play out your strategy. Crafty attorneys have developed legally defendable processes to get around the retaliatory prohibitions. These processes are well beyond the scope of this book.

It is sufficient to note that job eliminations are often couched with specific business purposes that are described in objective terms. The bottom line is that these myths are usually not successful in keeping you employed.

As you may recall, the company and your manager are in need of employees who are silent soldiers willing to do whatever it takes to help the company and the manager survive. Being labeled as something other than a "true company employee" makes it all but impossible for your manager to save your job. This is true regardless of how beneficial you are to your manager's job. By exercising your rights, you have sent out a completely contradictory message of how you want to be perceived to enhance your chances of remaining employed. In attempting to protect your job through a claim filing, you may have just moved yourself into the first wave of job eliminations.

Reality check:

- Question Number 1: Is it illegal to place an employee's name on the job elimination list solely because of a claim filing? Answer: YES.
- Question Number 2: Will the employee win a retaliatory discharge claim based on the company's actions in violation of the law? Answer: PROBABLY NOT (if the company's attorney is experienced in job eliminations).

Please do not interpret this as condoning a company's violation of an employee's rights. If, in fact, you sustained a work-related injury or are being discriminated against or harassed in the workplace, you should avail yourself of the proper channels to protect your rights. Unfortunately, during difficult economic times, employees with valid claims sometimes get snagged in the big net that the company casts to identify disenchanted employees for job elimination.

Rule of Thumb
By all means, exercise your legal rights when you see fit. However, you should be aware that filing a claim typically does not prevent you from losing your job in layoff situations regardless of the laws prohibiting retaliation.

CHAPTER 15

RECAP WITH A SIDE OF VARIABLES

As mentioned earlier, there is no cookie-cutter approach that can be universally applied to all scenarios to protect a job. There are simply too many variables that influence the outcome of any specific situation. The following are some examples of significant variables that commonly influence your job security more than the personality of your manager:

- The type of relationship you had with your manager prior to the economic downturn
- Where your salary falls within the compensation range for your position and how comparable your rate of pay is with your peers
- Whether you took an extended leave from work within the recent past regardless of the reason
- If you were formally disciplined in writing within the recent past
- Whether you have been verbally critical about the company's strategy since the economic downturn
- If you have been outwardly negative about the company's decision on previous job eliminations
- Whether you have an inside connection that helped you secure your position in the first place
- If you have a unique connection with a major customer that would quickly pull business away from the company if you were no longer working on that account
- If your position is covered by a collective bargaining agreement
- If you're a union steward or other recognized union representative at the company
- The size of your company

My goal has been accomplished if you understand that the

most important element to staying employed during an economic crisis is to perceive all developments from the vantage point of your manager. When you understand this, you can behave in a manner that is consistent with what is important to your manager—not with what is important to you or to the company. If you grasp this concept, you can vigilantly look out for your own best interests by applying it to your specific scenario.

In the next section, I discuss how you should plan on the worst while hoping for the best. In other words, you need to be proactive in protecting your interests just in case your job is eliminated. Being proactive will enable you to take advantage of information and reference materials found at your work that will be lost to you forever after your job elimination.

Rule of Thumb

While there are many variables that can impact an employee's specific situation at a specific company, there is one prevalent factor for everyone regardless of where they work. In developing a game plan to improve job security, you must make decisions from the perspective of your manager. Your opinion and the company's goals are extraneous.

PREPARING FOR THE WORST

CHAPTER 16

BE A BOY SCOUT

A true but adapted story:

Driving into work that frigid January morning it felt colder than usual in Chicago. I had the car heater blasting, yet I shivered. In hindsight, it had little to do with the warmth of the car and more to do with my feelings about that day's scheduled events. I was going to be involved in the job elimination of a senior member of management of a publicly traded company. This was nothing new for me. I had done it countless times before. Still, this time it was different.

You see, the target in the crosshairs of my rifle on that day was a friend. The two of us met for lunch twice a month for several years. Our lunch conversation typically started with work-related matters but inevitably turned to friendly banter about our personal lives. We had much in common. We each had four children. Through all the stories we shared, I understood his personal challenges and tribulations and felt as though I knew his family as well as my own. We had become confidants for each other.

There would be no lunch that day. There would be no friendly banter. It would go as I planned and had done hundreds of times before and subsequently. I would do the talking, and my soon-to-be ex-friend would stare in disbelief. There would be no anger. Anger is an emotion that is generally not experienced until after the shock of the news is dealt with.

When my friend arrived, I struggled to speak for the first time in my career. My words seemed to fight being said. Being a career hatchet man, the words did eventually come. That cold January day, I accomplished my job. I terminated an individual whom I still consider to this day to be a personal friend. Yes, he was certainly more than a professional peer.

The blank stare my friend wore on his face crippled me at my desk. The man who stood 6 feet 7 inches tall when he arrived at my office only moments before slumped over in my plush armchair and seemed to shrivel up. He said nothing. As tears welled up in his eyes, I wondered what he was thinking. Was he in shock that he lost his job? Was he in shock that I, his personal friend, committed such an unspeakable act and took away the paycheck that fed his family? The meeting lasted less than ten minutes, but it seemed to me—and I am sure to him—that astronauts had flown to the moon in less time.

I made an exception for my friend and allowed him to return to his office with me beside him. This would be the only time in my career that I escorted a terminated employee myself. After all, he deserved that respect from me. I would compare my state of mind at that point as roughly the equivalent of that when you attend a friend's funeral. No, it was even worse because I was the one who metaphorically killed him. I wanted so badly to take the cowardly route and have someone else escort him out. After what I had done to him, he deserved my compassion more than I deserved my own self-serving goal of avoiding the situation any further.

When we returned to his office, I realized that he had never planned for the worst. Although the company was in the midst of a nationwide restructuring, he never thought it would happen to him. His computer privileges were shut off during the meeting in my office, and everything he had stored over the years on his hard drive was gone. I am confident that he had reference materials saved on his computer that were not confidential. He could have copied and taken home the reference materials the day before without any concerns by the company. The opportunity was lost forever to him.

He noted that he did not have any telephone numbers written down because all his contacts were stored in his cell phone. Unfortunately, the cell phone belonged to the company and was now in my coat pocket. After about five minutes in his office, he said his farewells to his secretary. Keeping with protocol, he was not allowed to talk to his employees. I watched him carry a half-empty box of his possessions out to his car. The box was filled with nothing more than some personal pictures, mementos, and a plaque with a diamond shape on it. He received that plaque from the CEO the year before at an award banquet at which he was honored as one of the company's top ten employees worldwide.

***

Do Not Delay Preparation
Everyone has heard that the best way to find a new job is through networking. Many books have been written about it. While the concept is widely understood, I am surprised by how many people do not realize that the first stage of networking ideally starts while you are still employed.

Smart companies have the information technology department cancel an employee's computer rights during the employee's termination meeting. After the termination meeting, employees are only allowed to gather their physical belongings and depart. They are not allowed to make copies of anything, talk to fellow employees, or go back on their computer. Along with their company keys and swipe cards, individuals are required to immediately return their cell phones. As you can see, when you are called into a termination meeting, your sources of information for networking purposes vanish. This situation is completely avoidable with a little foresight.

At the first glimmer of tough times at work, you should prepare for the worst and hope for the best. Preparing for the worst includes commencing the first stages of networking in earnest. Effective networking includes compiling up-to-date contact information (all telephone numbers, addresses, e-mail addresses, current job titles) for pivotal individuals in your network. Pivotal individuals are those who can serve as a business or professional reference. These individuals can also serve as additional sets of eyes and ears looking for opportunities for you. Gathering this essential information is easy while you are still working at the company.

If you wait until after your job is eliminated to begin to network, you may find yourself in the situation where you are unable to locate company peers or external business associates who could have helped you. This can leave you without your network intact and can result in your spending valuable time trying to find these individuals. In large companies, you can take notes from the company phone directory of the names and telephone numbers of any and all individuals who can possibly help you should you be let go. In smaller companies, you can photocopy or print out the employee telephone directory. You should always error on the safe side and note the names of every individual you have worked with even if you can't fathom how they will ever be able to help you.

This list of names and telephone numbers must be stored at

home. If you are asked to leave, the company will not allow you to walk out with this information. Companies always fear that past employees will contact present employees in the future about job opportunities at the former employee's new company. When you are proactive in saving this data at home beforehand, you can walk right out the front door with the same information without anyone saying a word. If a manager does inquire into the reason you are taking the data home, you can simply reply that it may be necessary or helpful when you work from home. You additionally should make a copy of the employee handbook for your home. It may become necessary for an attorney to review the document should you seek a consultation regarding your employment rights if you are terminated.

There is another vital source of information that needs to be gathered from reference documents at your place of employment prior to your job elimination. This is specific information or details that will assist you in quantifying your accomplishments (i.e., cost savings, sales produced, participation percentages). As most recruiters, headhunters, or books that discuss preparing your résumé state, your accomplishments backed by quantifiable numbers pack a stronger punch than a simple listing of your job responsibilities. Therefore, you need to proactively reflect on your past accomplishments and take inventory of what you have achieved while still employed. From there, you can determine what information provides quantifiable support for each accomplishment and seek it out for purposes of completing your résumé.

I feel compelled at this point to remind you that anything that is confidential or a trade secret should never be removed from your place of employment without management's consent. Doing so without prior approval can be interpreted as a violation of federal or state law.

Rule of Thumb
When your company or the economy is struggling, you should hope for the best but plan for the worst. Be proactive, plan ahead, and copy everything at work that will be of use to you in a job search in case a job search becomes necessary.

CHAPTER 17

LISTEN, DON'T TALK

Let's start with an overview of what typically occurs during the employment termination meeting. You are called into an office or to a location where the meeting can be held with privacy. You may or may not be provided with a written document known as a severance package. The topic of severance packages is discussed later in this book. In addition to your immediate manager, there is generally one other company representative present at the meeting. More than likely, the other representative will be from the human resources department. The company representative serves as a witness to what occurs. This individual usually doesn't talk during the meeting but instead takes notes. The witness is for the benefit of the company not you, the terminated employee.

It's not a legal requirement that there be a witness present. However, there usually is one there. The sole purpose of the representative is to corroborate what is said during the meeting. In my experience, this individual tends to have selective memory and note taking skills in that the witness records your comments extensively but records very limited amounts of what the terminating manager says. In other words, the representative will corroborate what you say when you put your foot in your mouth and damage your potential claim. Don't plan on the company representative corroborating damaging statements that might have been mistakenly blurted out by an unprepared manager.

The role of the representative should be more accurately named "Company Witness 1" because the entire concept was created by company attorneys with an eye toward potential litigation. You would be amazed at the amount of litigation that stems from comments made by company managers during termination meetings. With the company representative now in the room, it is your statement against the two of theirs. Company attorneys are more than prepared to refute your claim that a comment made by the company manager was an admission that the termination was premised on an illegal purpose.

The Dos and Don'ts during a Termination Meeting

For the company, the less you know, the better it is from a legal perspective. Managers are trained to not disclose any details about how they made their decision to eliminate your position. Doing so opens the door to a discussion that they will never win with you. Thus, you generally are let go without specifics and without any justification for the decision. If the manager was trained well, the meeting will be brief, and your questions will go unanswered.

While it is only marginally successful, there is one technique to get some truth out of your manager and some answers to your questions. To accomplish this, you have to derail your manager off his or her scripted meeting notes and get your manager speaking from the top of his or her head and the bottom of his or her heart. This can be done by making the manager feel extremely uncomfortable. The most effective method I have observed for doing so is to stare blankly at your manager's face when he or she stops talking. I don't care how many times (s)he's terminated an employee or what type of personality or temperament your manager has, the termination meeting is a stressful and uncomfortable situation for her or him as well. The longer you sit there quietly, the more awkward it becomes. Inevitably, your manager will fill the awkward silence with nervous chatter. I cannot tell you how many times I needed to stop a nervous manager from talking too much. One caveat to the above suggestion is to avoid staring at your manager with an angry face. This look will result in the meeting ending abruptly, which is the opposite of your goal.

It is best for you to not say much either. There are no negotiations at the termination meeting. After your manager notifies you that your position has been eliminated, there is nothing you can say to change that decision. It is too late to try to implement any of the suggestions contained in this book. You should sit silently and try to retain what is said to you. Immediately afterwards, take detailed notes by answering reporter type questions concerning the meeting, including what, where, when, why, who, and how it played out. Jot down everything you remember. Do not use discretion or weed out information because something that seems unimportant then might become vital later. This is especially true should you consult with an attorney.

Anything you say at this time is primarily driven by emotion rather than intellect. You are unprepared, and your comments can be taken out of context. This fact is significant because the company witness will be taking notes during the meeting, and your manager will probably do so immediately after the meeting. Your documented comments made in anger, frustration, or confusion will assuredly not help you and may be used against you should you subsequently file a lawsuit against the company for its employment practices.

Additionally, your comments may result in the denial of your claim for state unemployment benefits. Many unemployed individuals have found themselves wishing that they had kept quiet during the termination meeting after reading the company's position statement fighting their unemployment claim. Save your final words for a discussion with an attorney, for your unemployment application, or for a complaint to be filed with an administrative agency or court. Don't waste your comments in a room where the audience is biased and unsympathetic. Save your comments for a more neutral setting where the merit of what you are saying will actually be heard.

Your quiet victory will come from knowing that you implemented the suggestions in this book and thus were prepared for the possibility of this event. In so doing, you widened your networking circle of contacts, expanded your skill set for your résumé, and safeguarded all information that will be necessary for your future job search. If you accomplished this, you are light years ahead of your peers who were terminated while still struggling in the zombie stage.

In the next section, I discuss topics that are relevant if you do suffer a job elimination. Specifically, a road map is offered that will prompt you to gather information in an expedited manner; help you understand your options, alternatives, and rights; and make informed decisions in a timely fashion.

Rule of Thumb

When being let go, listen carefully, ask questions, and ask for clarification if you don't understand something. Because emotions run high in these situations, the less you talk, the better off you are. Last but not least, take written notes immediately after the meeting.

THE WORST IS HERE

CHAPTER 18

PREVENTING COMPANY EXPLOITATION

You developed a strategy and skillfully played it out, but you were let go nonetheless. What do you do next? My focus here is not on providing guidance on finding your next job but on how to handle the critical and time-sensitive matters that occur as a result of your job termination. If you let the typical emotions that accompany a job loss (such as denial, anger, and depression) take over, you will compound your losses by depriving yourself of the critical time necessary to make informed decisions. You must resist these unconstructive emotions and aggressively use the limited time you are provided by law to gather information, understand your alternatives, and move on your informed decisions.

The critical decisions that need to be made regarding your previous employment too often are ignored. They compete for your time with your need to find new employment and time to waddle in self-pity. These competing interests and emotions work to the company's best interests. In a bad economy, you may be unemployed longer than anticipated. Therefore, it is foolish to only look forward and not protect yourself by maximizing what is rightfully owed to you by your previous employer. You need to act, and you need to act fast before your options and alternatives offered by or against your past company disappear forever. This section discusses what your options are, and it provides a system to ensure that you make timely and informed decisions.

Emotional Rollercoaster

Being out of work is one of the most overwhelming experiences an individual can face. This is particularly true during an economic downturn where there is a significant possibility that you may be out of work for a substantial period of time. There is no time to waste feeling sorry for yourself or bearing a grudge against your past company. Your landlord, mortgage lender, and credit card companies don't care about what occurred but rather when they will get paid.

Granted, advice is easier to give than to receive, but as a seasoned business lawyer in these matters, this advice is truly priceless. The brief window for you to act intelligently and in the best interests of yourself and your dependents starts the day of your termination. As discussed later in this book, the window of time is very short. In some situations, it is measured in weeks, not years. The life cycle of your legal rights, each of which has a different time frame, is comparable to a starburst in the sky. It starts as a raging ball of fire (resembling the plethora of rights at your disposal) and ceases with a mere, final flicker of light (when the statute of limitations on your last legal right expires).

Within a matter of weeks of your termination, you are inundated with documents that involve your legal rights. You will receive notices from your company, health insurance provider, 401(k) plan, etc. These complicated notices explain your legal rights and contain short deadlines for action. If you fail to act in a timely manner, your legal rights begin slipping away. For the most part, they cannot be revived. It borders on cruelty that you're forced to make important decisions on matters that are foreign to you on an expedited time frame while you're still reeling from losing your job. The law is clear in providing these deadlines, so you have no choice. The next few chapters will hopefully provide you with some comfort in making these decisions.

It is imperative that you remember that you and your company are adversaries at this point in time. You are on your own. Unlike when you started with the company, the human resources department will not call you with reminders about the paperwork that is due. No company representative will call you and explain what the paperwork means. You will not receive a second notice or a past due notice. No one will remind you that you are about to lose all your rights against the company.

The company prefers that you not respond. In fact, the only reason the company or its vendors sent you the documentation in the first place is because it is mandated under federal and state law. Your deadlines are nothing more than a notation on the calendar of the human resources department and an entry in the journal of the company's attorney—deadlines that they hope pass without hearing from you.

Rule of Thumb
Although losing your job is emotionally challenging, you must control your emotions to effectively make informed decisions on important issues with short deadlines that are the result of the job termination.

CHAPTER 19

RUM IS THE ANSWER

As discussed in the previous chapter, when you are terminated from your position, there are many competing interests for your time. You are preparing your résumé, looking for job opportunities, networking, fine-tuning your elevator speech, and lining up your references. The list goes on and on. The one thing that needs to be on your list of action items and marked as urgent is how to wrap up your past employment. This action item can ultimately have more impact on your future than the résumés you are sending out. By wrapping up your past employment, I mean that you don't move on without first understanding what you are leaving behind.

I have always marveled at how company's control the amount of knowledge that individuals learn about the employment relationship. Through their human resources departments, companies teach employees how to perform their jobs, how to select their health benefits, and how to be noticed for promotions. An employee's lifeline to all key decisions in the employment relationship goes back to the company. The company is viewed as knowledgeable, supportive, and fair. But what do you do when you are let go and the relationship ends? Now, the company that you relied on for information is your adversary, and it strives to give you as little information as possible. In the next three chapters, I walk you through a system that you can use as a road map to help you answer difficult questions.

In this chapter, I point out what the company intentionally never explained to you about the employment relationship. For starters, the company's obligations to you are not dead on your last day of work. On the contrary, it arguably has more obligations to you after your termination. These obligations are short-lived and must be understood and acted on swiftly. In general terms, you need to quickly assess the following points at the end of your employment relationship so that you can determine how to proceed:

- Will your previous employer provide you with a positive reference to any potential employer?

- What opportunities did your past company extend to you that are advantageous?
- What are your legal rights against your previous employer?

Anything you want or expect from your past company needs to be addressed within a short time frame of your termination while your rights are still enforceable. When you walk out the door after your termination meeting, you have more leverage against the company at that point in time than you ever had in the past or ever will in the future. Yet, terminated employees generally do nothing more than shrug their shoulders and mistakenly believe there is nothing they can do. If you or someone you know has thought this, then you may want to get out a highlighter before reading the next three chapters.

The reason for the urgency is based on the length of time that it takes to compile the documents necessary to understand your options and make an informed decision. In some instances, there are more specific reasons for the urgency, and they will be explained when appropriate. After finishing the following three chapters, you should be able to answer these important questions:

- Why do you need to review your personnel file?
- What should you do if you disagree with something in your personnel file?
- How can you learn specifics about your legal rights?
- What should you know before selecting an attorney?
- What legal avenues and remedies are available to you if your rights were violated?
- Were you entitled to a severance package?
- Can you be required to sign a severance document or waiver to receive your last payroll check?
- What is your leverage in asking your past company for severance pay or for a better severance package?
- Should you sign the severance package offered?
- What is the significance of signing a severance document?
- What happens to your health insurance coverage under the company plan when your employment is terminated?
- What is the purpose of the COBRA notice?
- Why your previous employer will not provide you with additional time to make a decision about COBRA

coverage?

- Can the cost of COBRA exceed the amount actually paid while you were an active employee?
- How do you know if the company health insurance plan is worth the cost?
- When do you have to make a decision about whether you will continue to participate in the company health insurance plan?

I have a simple system to help you answer these questions in an intelligent and timely manner. The system is: **RUM**. Sure, you can drink it, but that's not going to really help anything, is it? RUM is an acronym for the system that you can utilize as a road map following termination. RUM stands for the following:

- **REQUEST**. Request and compile all documentation and information necessary for you to understand your options.
- **UNDERSTAND**. Understand your options, and if you don't, consult with an attorney, and then make informed decisions.
- **MOVE**. Move on your informed decisions expeditiously because time is of the essence.

Each of these three steps is discussed in greater detail and is the topic of its own chapter.

Rule of Thumb
The company's obligations to you do not stop the day you are let go. But because the company's interests are diametrically opposed to yours at that point, the company must be viewed as your adversary. Use the RUM system to request information, understand your options, and make timely decisions in protecting your interests.

CHAPTER 20
STEP 1: REQUEST

Before you can understand your options and make informed and timely decisions, you need to compile the information that is essential to the decision-making process. There are two primary sources of information that you need to obtain and review to make informed decisions: your personnel file and comparative quotes on health insurance.

Personnel File

The first day after your employment termination you should request in writing a copy of your personnel file. The request should be sent to the attention of the human resources department and delivered via certified mail return receipt requested. This method ensures that even an unscrupulous company will respond in a timely fashion. The laws of your state will dictate how long the company has to respond to your request, but it is generally within two weeks of receipt of your letter. I additionally suggest contacting the human resources department to see if there is an internal form for requesting a copy of the personnel file that you could complete to speed up the process. Either way, you should direct the company to contact you by telephone when the file is ready for pickup or review.

While your specific state determines your rights to the file, you typically are allowed to either review the file or copy the file. As a terminated employee, you need to quickly gain access to or possession of your personnel file for numerous reasons to be explained later. It is suffice to simply note that you have a limited period of time to assess whether your legal rights were violated and, if so, to file a claim to enforce your rights. An accurate assessment of whether your rights were honored is difficult, if not impossible, without reviewing your personnel file.

Additionally, if you received a severance package from your company when your employment was terminated, you probably were allowed a specific number of days to accept the document. In most situations, you are allowed twenty-one days to accept the package. If you were let go as part of a group or class of employees, you were probably provided forty-five days to accept the document. Regardless of whether you were given twenty-one or forty-five days to accept, you will be provided at least seven days following your acceptance to change your mind and revoke the agreement. The amount of time your company allows you to sign is not arbitrarily chosen out of thin air. It is the shortest time period that a company can provide you with when seeking to obtain a permanent waiver of your legal rights. Any shorter amount of time violates federal law, and your acceptance will not be deemed to have waived your rights regardless of whether you signed the document. An overview of your legal rights and protections stemming from your employment relationship with the company are enumerated in the next chapter.

Your only goal at this point is to review or copy your personnel file. You should not sign a severance document without first doing this and moving on to step 2 (Understand) of the RUM system. With that said, you need to get your hands on your personnel file as soon as possible because you only have either twenty-one or forty-five days to make your decision.

Health Insurance

If you participated in a company health plan, you will receive a notice of your rights to continue to participate in the health plan despite your job termination. This letter is referred to as a COBRA notice. Depending on the company's professionalism and organizational skills, you may receive the COBRA notice at the termination meeting. If not, you will receive it shortly afterward in the mail. There are many provisions in the COBRA notice that must be understood for you to make an informed decision. The details of the COBRA notice will be explained in step 2 (Understand) of the RUM system.

At the request stage of the RUM system, you need to perform preliminary legwork to be assured that you will be able to understand your options and make an informed decision in a timely manner. The legwork that is being referenced here involves obtaining comparative quotes of premium rates from other health insurance plans. The quotes serve as reference material to assist you in determining if COBRA coverage is the right choice for you.

Start by submitting a request for a health insurance quote from several insurance providers via the Internet. All that is needed for a free and instantaneous quote is the following information: the number of people to be covered, the sex and age of each person to be covered, and the plan design. Do not be intimidated by the phrase "plan design." Plan design for you, as compared to a company, is relatively simple. It basically involves choosing from the following options offered by health insurance companies:

- Whether you want a PPO or an HMO
- The dollar amount or percentage you will be responsible for when it comes to the co-pay and deductible
- Whether you want a prescription card

The Web sites of health insurance companies invariably include a link from each option listed above to a layman's description of the term. These sites explain the difference between a PPO and an HMO, and they define what a co-pay, a deductible, and a prescription card are in layman's terms. Unless you have special needs, such as pregnancy coverage, the health insurance plans that companies offer only differ in their amount of coverage for the terms mentioned above. You simply have to select the plan that best meets your anticipated needs.

Health insurance companies are not very creative with their plan designs, and they offer almost identical plans. This is good news for you because it requires less time to compare premium quotes on an apple-to-apple basis. You should start by choosing a plan design that most closely resembles your company-sponsored health plan. Because the quotes are free and there is no obligation to purchase, you should also explore different plan designs that may better fit your needs to determine if this results in a lower premium.

It is important to gather this information immediately because you will need to submit paperwork on the medical health of you and your dependents should you decide to further pursue another health insurance company. The new health insurance company will verify the medical status of you and your dependents by checking with your physicians. The verification process takes approximately three weeks. Remember, you are not in a position to switch health insurance companies until you receive written confirmation from the health insurance company that you submitted the medical health paperwork to that it will extend coverage to you under the plan design selected and for the premium quoted. Thus, you should begin to compile information to help you understand your health care options immediately after your employment termination. There is no reason to delay your request for comparative quotes until receipt of the COBRA notice. When you're in possession of the COBRA notice and reference materials from other health insurance companies, you are prepared to move to step 2 (Understand) of the RUM system.

Rule of Thumb
The first step in protecting your interests and ensuring that the company gave you everything you're entitled to is to gather all relevant documents. Because deadlines for making decisions are short, the documents need to be requested immediately. The documents are vital to understanding your options against the company as well as viable health insurance alternatives to COBRA.

CHAPTER 21

STEP 2: UNDERSTAND

The second step of the RUM system involves understanding the significance of the documents that you have requested and received and the laws that apply to them. When they are understood, the documents offer you options and avenues that are commonly overlooked by an overwhelmed, unemployed individual whose sole priority is finding another job. These options must be reviewed and considered immediately because they have a short shelf life and have built–in, unforgiving deadlines.

Recruiters, headhunters, and outplacement representatives advise displaced employees to take their experiences from the past and move forward with a positive attitude in their job search. While the advice sounds fundamentally valid, there is no justification for the individual to move forward blindly without understanding what is being left behind. It is nonsensical to consciously choose to be naïve and think that everything always works out well. Go to your local library any weekday morning, and ask the adults going through the Dun & Bradstreet reports how long they have been unemployed. Stand outside a bankruptcy courtroom, and listen to the heartbreaking stories of how long some individuals have been unemployed and how they are consequently losing their homes. Most of these individuals lost their jobs through no fault of their own.

The point is not to scare you but to stress that you should not ignorantly walk away from any legal rights or options that stem from your prior employment. You should first understand what you are entitled to and then make informed decisions. A prudent individual hopes for the best (finding gainful employment in the near term) but plans for the worst (the possibility of being displaced from the workforce for an extended period of time).

While each of the following topics could be a book in itself, I will highlight in this section the significant aspects of each of the following elements that you need to understand:

- your personnel file
- health insurance
- COBRA deadlines
- COBRA costs
- severance documents
- your legal rights

Your Personnel File

Upon receipt of or access to your personnel file, review it and determine if it is intact. The file is equivalent to a biography about your career at the company. Everything in the file should be accurate. This file can help or haunt you for the remainder of your career. More than likely, future companies will inquire into your previous employment and will contact your past employers to learn more about you. If your state does not require your company to provide you with a copy of the file, then be prepared to take notes when you go to review it. Take written notes of anything that is inaccurate and be specific and detailed so that you are able to reference any inaccuracies very clearly at a later date.

Companies are generally instructed by their attorneys to only provide limited information about past employees. This advice is based on fear that an inadvertent, slanderous comment may be made, resulting in a libel or defamation lawsuit. These same corporate attorneys have also developed ways around this roadblock for their business clients who are looking to gather information about potential employees from past employers. One such method works as follows: the hiring company knows that your past employer is generally required to provide you with access to or a copy of your personnel file when requested. Therefore, the human resources department of the company you are interviewing with asks you to obtain information directly from your past company on their behalf. Specifically, the main documents that the new company wants to see are the copies of your past performance reviews. Performance reviews are telling documents about an employee's work ethic and productivity.

Your personnel file or notes about inaccuracies in it are invaluable to an attorney should you seek legal advice on the circumstances surrounding your job elimination and your corresponding rights. It allows an attorney to get a clear picture of your employment history with the company. Over the years, I have been consulted by numerous relatives, friends, and the like for an opinion on their legal rights after a job elimination. To my amazement, I can count on one hand the number of individuals whose memory was 100 percent accurate and in agreement with their personnel file. An individual going through a job transition after termination is full of stress, and unproductive emotions can cloud his or her objectivity.

The personnel file or your notes therefrom additionally allow an attorney to figuratively peek into the backroom of your old company and begin to piece together what occurred and the motives behind the company's actions. It also provides a snapshot of the quality of the work product of the human resources department. If the work product is poor, there is a greater likelihood that a mistake will be found in the termination process, resulting in liability to the company.

Companies are known to place memos or unsigned documents into a personnel file. Therefore, there is a strong possibility that documents you never saw are in your personnel file. If there is something in your file that you do not agree with, never saw before, or are uncomfortable with, you should request that it be removed. The success of your request will depend ultimately on your leverage. Leverage comes in different shapes and forms and is based on many variables, including the lack of sophistication of the company's human resources department and the company's tolerance level for litigation. If you were asked to sign a severance document, you should demand that any paperwork in your personnel file with which you take exception be removed before you sign. You may not be successful in your requests or demands, but you will never know how much leverage you have until you ask. It is better to ask and be denied than not to ask at all.

Health Insurance Overview

If your company offered a health benefit plan, it is legally required to offer you the opportunity to continue in the plan for a specified period of time after your employment ceases with the company. The benefit laws that govern your rights in this situation are contained within the Consolidated Omnibus Budget Reconciliation Act, or COBRA for short.

The company is obligated to provide you with a copy of your COBRA rights upon your termination. If you do not receive this COBRA notice, you should contact the company and ask for it.

Then, send a letter via certified mail return receipt requested asking for the same. The letter will get their attention because there are statutory penalties for each day they fail to provide you with the COBRA notice after a short grace period.

COBRA Deadlines

The COBRA notice will expressly state the deadlines for any action required on your part if you decide to continue in your company's health insurance benefit plan. Specifically, the notice advises you of the deadline for electing to continue the coverage and the deadline for paying the premiums. Additionally, the notice will state where the documents and premiums should be mailed. Companies frequently delegate their responsibility for administering health insurance benefits for past employees to outside vendors who specialize in the complexities of COBRA.

COBRA administration is a negative drain on the most valuable resources of companies (i.e., time and money). Without question, companies only offer COBRA because it is mandated by law. Companies contend that they are unfairly required by law to assume the responsibility of administering a technical statute for the benefit of an individual they terminated. They additionally complain that they should not run the risk of liability exposure if they fall short of their legal obligations while administering COBRA. Nonetheless, liability exposure is there, and willful violations of COBRA by a company are punishable with severe legal consequences.

In early 2009, in response to the economic downturn, Congress passed an economic stimulus package (technically called the American Recovery and Reinvestment Act), temporarily modifying COBRA in favor of laid-off workers. The economic stimulus package requires companies to notify employees who were laid off as far back as September 1, 2008, that the company is required to absorb a significant portion of the monthly COBRA premium. This requirement is great for you, but it is a nightmare for the company from the standpoint of administration and accounting. With that said, companies loathe COBRA more today than ever before.

Companies and their attorneys are constantly looking for loopholes to avoid this responsibility. To date, none of any significance have been found. The only safe way for companies to skirt this obligation is to enforce the COBRA deadlines. Companies are not required to be flexible with missed deadlines and do not make exceptions to the dates set forth in the COBRA notice. You must treat COBRA deadlines as though they are written in stone.

COBRA Costs

You will probably react like everyone else in your situation and be shocked when you see the amount of your monthly health insurance premium. When you were an active employee, the company paid the majority portion of your monthly premium for health insurance. The portion paid by you was relatively small in comparison. Because your employee contribution was taken directly out of your paycheck as a payroll deduction, you probably never thought about your payment or how much was paid by the company. As a terminated employee, you are responsible for paying the entire monthly health insurance premium if you elect to continue COBRA coverage under the company health plan. COBRA does not require the company to continue to subsidize the costs of your health coverage unless you were laid off during the period after September 1, 2008, but before December 31, 2009. If your termination occurs during that specific period, the economic stimulus package requires your company to provide a subsidy payment on your behalf. More specifics about this situation are explained later in this section.

Depending on how your company viewed its workforce and many other factors, including whether you were in a union environment, determines how much your monthly health benefit contribution as a terminated employee will increase. It is not uncommon for the monthly premium for continuation of health coverage under COBRA to be more than 300 to 400 percent higher than the amount you paid prior to your termination. To add salt to the wound, COBRA allows the company to add an additional 2 percent to the overall monthly premium to cover its costs of handling the COBRA paperwork.

It is important that you understand that the premium under COBRA is higher than the premium you paid while employed. You will be solely responsible for the monthly premium noted in the COBRA notice. Only after you understand this can you intelligently compare your COBRA rates with the premium quotes from other health insurance companies on an even basis.

As previously mentioned, the economic stimulus package is a gift to laid-off employees because it shifts a significant portion of the monthly COBRA premium cost back to the company (who ultimately is reimbursed by the federal government). Specifically, the cost of

COBRA is paid 65 percent by the company and 35 percent by the employee. The amount paid by the company is typically referred to as a subsidy. Although this law was not passed until early 2009, the subsidy applies to employees who were laid off or will be laid off between the period of September 1, 2008, and December 31, 2009. If the economic stimulus package is not extended, the previous rules of COBRA will go back into effect on January 1, 2010, and apply to anyone laid off on that date or after.

Is COBRA Right for You?

Whether signing up for COBRA is right for you is a question that will be driven by your own personal circumstances. There are many factors that you should take into consideration. The following are several questions for you to think about and to answer realistically:

- How long do you think it will take you to find another job?
- How long will the waiting period be before you are eligible for health coverage at a new job? (Some companies offer immediate health coverage as of the first day of work; others require a new employee to work ninety days prior to coverage taking effect to coincide with a probationary period. Often, there is a norm for companies in specific industries.)
- What are the chances that your new employer will not offer a company-sponsored health benefit plan? (In poor economic times, many small and midsize businesses do not provide a company health plan.)
- What is the medical status of you and the dependents that you cover under your health insurance plan? (In some situations, it may be prudent for you to remain under COBRA because of preexisting health issues. The unfavorable medical status of anyone you provide health coverage for may make the premiums of a replacement health plan cost prohibitive or even impossible to find.)

As you can see, there is no universal right or wrong in deciding whether to continue COBRA health coverage through your previous employer. It may ease your mind to remember that if you elect to continue coverage and subsequently find a more affordable health plan, you can always cancel COBRA going forward. On the other hand, your decision to not take COBRA coverage, is permanent should you change your mind and subsequently want it.

Severance Documents Overview

Companies generally have a low threshold for litigation risk. This fact is exacerbated by corporate attorneys who routinely advise their clients that federal and state laws governing employment matters, including benefits, tend to favor employees over the company. Moreover, because employment laws are extremely complicated and constantly changing, it is virtually impossible for human resources personnel to keep abreast of the current state of the law. Therefore, companies try to minimize their liability exposure by offering terminated employees something of value in return for signing a waiver of their rights to file a lawsuit against the company.

To persuade disgruntled, terminated employees to permanently waive their rights to sue the company, corporate lawyers developed a special enticement known as the severance package. In its simplest sense, a severance package has two parts: (1) the benefit to you and (2) the benefit to the company. The benefit to you is that the company will give you something you are not otherwise entitled to. The benefit offered in return for signing a release may be a certain amount of money, outplacement services, and continued subsidized health benefits for a limited duration after your termination.

The signed release is the benefit to the company. *Release*, in this sense, is a legal term that means an express waiver of your legal rights to sue the company for anything that occurred during your employment. Corporate lawyers draft releases to be extremely broad, so you should assume that you will lose your ability to ever sue the company if you sign one.

Your Right to a Severance Package

Merely being employed by a company does not entitle you to a severance package upon job termination. For there to be a right, it must be provided by contract or law. In larger companies, employee handbooks frequently state that an employee experiencing a job elimination is entitled to severance pay. Severance pay is typically expressed in terms of a specified number of weeks of pay that is directly correlated to the number of years the employee worked for the company. The employee handbook will additionally note that the pay is contingent on the employee signing the company severance package. The company severance package always contains the release described above.

Sometimes companies offer severance packages even when the law does not require it and when the employee handbook is silent on the issue. In this situation, please note that the company can legally revoke the severance document anytime before you sign it. Because the sole purpose of offering the severance package in the first place is to prevent litigation risk, it is highly unusual for companies to revoke the severance document. A signed severance package provides the company with the comfort of knowing that any mistakes made in the employment relationship will not come back to haunt them.

With the dynamics of today's global marketplace and the increasing pressure on businesses to show profits, companies are responding with a quick but temporary fix. In difficult economic times, companies often respond by eliminating jobs. Job eliminations accompanied by severance pay are expensive; therefore, severance pay language in employee handbooks is becoming less common. Companies want to keep their options open and determine at a later date whether it will extend severance packages. I am confident that severance pay language in employee handbooks will eventually become as rare as company-sponsored pension plans, which were universally found less than thirty years ago.

Severance Pay Is Different Than Earned Pay

Unreputable or uninformed companies sometimes state that you will not get your last paycheck for the wages you earned for work performed unless you sign a waiver of your rights. In this situation, the company attempts to transform your pay into severance pay. While laws differ in every state, they are consistent with the position that companies must pay discharged employees for wages earned. A company that refuses to pay your earned wages unless you sign a severance document is acting in an illegal manner. Companies that try this tactic—and there are quite a few—commonly require you to sign the severance document the day you are terminated. Employees in this situation are usually told that the offer is revoked if they don't sign the severance document that day. The company uses pressure tactics to persuade you to sign while your emotions are running rampant and when you have not had a chance to consult with a lawyer about your rights.

Your Federal and State Employment Rights

The simple act of signing a release with your old company that provides some form of benefit you are not otherwise entitled to effectively extinguishes any rights that you may have had under the plethora of federal and state laws. While signing a severance package may be a good deal in some situations, you should not do so until you have a sufficient understanding of your rights to make an informed decision.

Companies utilize language in their communications with their workforces that helps them avoid liability down the road. The most prevalent language used by companies is the verbiage *at will employee* or some variation of the same. Corporate attorneys and human resources personnel use this terminology frequently to subconsciously convince employees that they have virtually no legal rights in the workplace. While it is accurate to note that many states have laws that consider employees to be employed at will unless the company states otherwise, your rights in the workplace do not stop there. In fact, nothing could be further from the truth.

While employment at will means the company can terminate your employment, it does not mean that it can do so for any reason with impunity. There is a large body of federal and state laws that govern every part of the employment relationship, including job eliminations. If the company violates any of these laws, it is at risk that you may seek monetary damages. Enumerated below are some of the complicated federal laws that were enacted to protect you, the employee, and that govern the employment relationship:

- ADEA (Age Discrimination in Employment Act)
- ADA (Americans with Disabilities Act)
- Title VI and Title VII of the Civil Rights Act
- EEO (Equal Employment Opportunity)
- FLSA (Fair Labor Standards Act)
- USERRA (Uniformed Services Employment and Reemployment Rights Act)
- NLRA (National Labor Relations Act)
- Wage and Hour laws
- OSHA (Occupational Safety and Health Act)
- HIPAA (Health Insurance Portability and Accountability Act)
- ERISA (Employee Retirement Income Security Act)

- WARN Act (Worker Adjustment and Retraining Notification Act)
- COBRA (Consolidated Omnibus Budget Reconciliation Act)
- ARRA (American Recovery and Reinvestment Act of 2009)

Each of these federal laws protects separate and distinct rights you have as an employee regardless of whether you are an at will employee. Additionally, every state has its own version of these laws. Your rights under these laws survive the job elimination but only for a short period.

All federal and state laws have a drop-dead cutoff date for you to enforce your rights. This cutoff date is known as the statute of limitations. The statute of limitations is different for each law. The statute of limitations is harsh and brutal by nature to the employee, but it is only fair to allow the company to close its terminated employment files at some point in time. No matter how valid your claim is or how egregious the conduct of your previous employer was, the courts will dismiss your claim if you do not initiate your lawsuit by the deadline provided in the federal or state law. Deadlines can be quite short. In some situations, they are measured in weeks.

A more detailed discussion of the governing employment laws is beyond the scope of this book. My goal has been achieved if you understand that there are numerous protections afforded to you by federal and state laws regardless of whether your company states that you're an at will employee. With very little time investment, you can learn more about the general protections of each law via the Internet. If you think you have a claim but are not sure, you should consult with an attorney who handles employment matters.

Attorneys and Self-Representation

When scheduling a face-to-face appointment with an employment attorney to review your rights, you should always make sure that the initial consultation is free. Bring your personnel file, the company employee handbook, the termination letter if one was provided, and any severance documents to the meeting. The attorney will grasp your scenario more quickly and will have more time to talk to you about your rights if you draw a timeline of the significant events during the course of your employment with that company in advance. Significant events would include your hire/

termination date, dates of changes in your pay rate, date of last raise, promotion/demotion dates, date of last performance review, names of direct managers and the periods you reported to each of them, and dates of any disciplinary write-ups.

If you decide to retain an attorney to prosecute your claim, you should insist that the attorney you select work on a contingency fee basis. Avoid an attorney who charges hourly fees regardless of outcome. The contingency fee arrangement more closely aligns the attorney to your side because there is no attorney fee payout unless you win.

Another topic that also needs to be discussed when retaining an attorney is responsibility for the expenses and costs incurred during the litigation. Costs and expenses take the form of court costs, deposition and travel expenses, copying costs, and the like. These out-of-pocket expenses add up to thousands of dollars very quickly, especially if expert witnesses need to be used. A seasoned attorney should be able to give you an estimate of expenses based on the nature and facts of your case. In the absence of any agreement otherwise, the attorney may seek reimbursement from you. The retention/engagement letter prepared by the attorney will explain the services that will be provided for you. This letter should include the circumstances in which attorney fees will be paid and who will be responsible for the payment of costs and expenses as the case proceeds.

If you want to protect your rights on your own, the Equal Employment Opportunity Commission and its state agency counterparts that protect employee rights are very helpful with inquiries from individuals. They have user friendly Web sites and toll-free numbers to call for guidance and information. The Equal Employment Opportunity Commission also has help desks staffed with representatives who will assist you in preparing a complaint against your past company.

Rule of Thumb
To protect your interests, you must understand your options. After reviewing the relevant documents you requested, you should have a better understanding of your choices. Seek guidance from a professional advisor on any issues you feel you don't have a grasp of after reviewing the documentation.

CHAPTER 22

STEP 3: MOVE
(ON YOUR DECISIONS)

At this point, you did everything you could to understand the situation, including consulting an attorney if necessary. You have a thorough understanding of your options and alternatives and a basic understanding of your legal rights. All options and alternatives are still available because you performed the first two steps of the RUM system in an expeditious manner. You now need to determine what the best action is for your specific circumstances and communicate that decision to the relevant party (i.e., company, health insurance carrier, state agency, attorney you will retain). Thus, you are at the third step of the RUM system.

As mentioned throughout this section, when you lose your job, there are many issues that you need to explore and understand. Many of these issues are governed by laws that contain short deadlines. These deadlines are real and must be respected. There are no extensions on the deadlines for confusion, ignorance, or inadvertent failure to act on your decisions. These deadlines must be marked on your calendar, and they are every bit as important as an interview date. Your failure to be fully prepared on the marked date can result in outcomes even more tragic than those associated with going into an interview unprepared.

No one at your old company will seek you out for your decision. After all, your decision may not be in the company's best interests. Whether you fail to make a decision or fail to communicate the same, a decision has been made. In situations with statutory deadlines, your indecision constitutes a decision not to proceed. Don't let fear or neglect stop you from communicating your informed and reasoned decision. Control your destiny, communicate your informed decisions in writing, and keep a copy as proof of the communication.

Rule of Thumb

Procrastination works to the benefit of the company. Act swiftly in requesting information and understanding your options and legal rights. Then, communicate your informed decision in a timely manner.

EPILOGUE

A true story that unfortunately is not adapted:

Call it what you may: restructuring, reorganization, reduction in workforce (RIF), downsizing, business realignment, redirection, rightsizing, or any other flavor of the month. I have been responsible for planning and implementing all of the above. However, the hatchet man has also learned some lessons the hard way when it comes to job eliminations. Specifically, the company's figurative gun always has one bullet left in the chamber. You see, I too was left for dead one time when an unknown sniper from out of town met me at my office door. She advised me that my most successful nationwide restructuring was not complete because I was still there. Ouch!

***

For those of you who are presently or will be soon battling me or one of my peers in the job market, I wish you the best.

For those of you who have already fallen victim to a job elimination, I can empathize with you, having been in your situation myself.

For those of you who question the validity and necessity of a consulting field that specializes in job eliminations, I share the above true story. I hope the irony brings a smile to your face.

www.ingramcontent.com/pod-product-compliance
Lightning Source LLC
Chambersburg PA
CBHW050405290526
45786CB00003B/1135